THE VERSATILE SHED

HOW TO BUILD, RENOVATE AND CUSTOMIZE YOUR BONUS SPACE

CHRIS GLEASON

B

BETTERWAY HOME
CINCINNATI, OHIO
WWW.BETTERWAYBOOKS.COM

TABLE OF
CONTENTS

INTRODUCTION

I'm not sure exactly when the first house was built, but my guess is that it was probably followed a short time later by the first shed. People have always constructed small outbuildings as a way to gain additional space, whether it is for working or storage, and this need is as vital today as ever. Today's challenging housing market means that it is difficult for a lot of folks to trade up, so many of us are finding creative ways to make our current homes do more. One of my favorite ways to do this is by considering the value that a shed or small outbuilding might add to your daily life. Formerly just a place to store the lawnmower, sheds have undergone a bit of a renaissance in the past few years: the phrase "shed working" has entered our collective lexicon, and the tiny house movement has perfectly illustrated that a high quality of life can be attained with very little space, indeed.

Because I believe so strongly in the potential that sheds have to offer us — as fun, creative, and interesting bonus spaces — I have written this book in a way that I hope addresses a lot of different perspectives. For those who would like to build their own sheds, I have offered step-by-step construction photos and tips. For readers who would like to modify an existing shed to meet their needs, I think that there is a lot of great info on how to do just that. And finally, for everyone, including those who are just looking for some inspiration to show what's possible, I have assembled a lot of beautiful pictures of sheds that just about anybody would be proud to have in their yard.

Here's to a great shed project!
Christopher Gleason

Salt Lake City, Utah
November 24, 2011

CHAPTER ONE

Off-The-Rack Sheds

If you're not interested in building your own shed, you'll probably end up working with a company in your area that specializes in small outbuildings. I spent some time with Mike Anderson from A-Sheds, a company with offices in both Denver and Salt Lake City, and I was really impressed with what they have to offer. I took a tour of a number of different models that they had on hand, and learned a lot about some of the more unique projects that they've undertaken. Mike affirmed my belief that sheds can be much more than just a place to store the lawn mower. Their company has built sheds that have been transformed into:

Art studios
Pottery studios
Motorcycle garage
Small rec rooms
Offices
and Mini-Cabins

I think that this photo tour will demonstrate the kind of quality and attention to detail that you may be able to expect.

Mike had my attention right away when he directed me toward this unassuming looking building: it contains the office of one of their salesmen. (As an aside, Mike said that they're building a lot of sheds with porches now, too. His clients seem to like the looks and the fact that it creates a nice shady place to set up an outdoor area for seating and entertaining).

This shed demonstrates perfectly the way that a small outbuilding can go above and beyond. This office (left) lacks nothing in terms of being a comfortable and efficient place to work. There is even ample space to meet with prospective clients and roll out a set of blueprints. (above)

Even though I visited on a chilly day in late Autumn, the interior was cozy thanks to this electric baseboard heater.

I loved the cedar shakes below the eaves. It turns out that custom paint/trim jobs like this are very popular.

Mike mentioned that they have seen a real increase in demand for playhouses — this one caught my eye as being both very solidly built and also rather cute with the custom cupola on the roof.

There is so much vertical space, in fact, that most of their clients end up wanting a small loft to create an upstairs bedroom or a children's play area. If you are lucky enough to have a blank canvas like this, I imagine that you could come up with all kinds of cool interior treatments and finishes.

Mike told me that they built 50 of these mini cabins this year. The interiors can be left wide open so that the owners can customize them, or they can be fully built out with insulation, drywall, and paint. The gambrel-style roof provides nearly 16' of uninterrupted height at its peak. You could just about have a small basketball court in there.

This trim detailing definitely goes above and beyond. The window is also made with double-paned, insulated glass, which means that it would be very energy efficient if you chose to insulate and heat the interior.

I was impressed by their doors: they feature a steel frame for rigidity, which makes it nearly impossible to break in.

The steel frame was carefully engineered to allow the opportunity to use conventional locking handsets. This provides a lot of security, and it also gives you the option of choosing just about any exterior lockset that you like.

The interior of their sheds can be kept cool in the summer with the addition of these baffles that reflect heat up through the vented ridge cap. I'd be interested in trying these myself.

A-Sheds constructs their foundations from 2x6 galvanized steel beams. This means that the part of the shed that contacts the ground is especially well protected from water damage. It also allows them to confidently offer a 10-year warranty.

Profile on Mike Olfert from OutsideUp

Mike Olfert builds, in my opinion, some of the most beautiful sheds in the country. Here's some background on his work, in his own words:

"I live in Portland, and have lived in Oregon all my life. I was a magazine photographer for some years when I realized that my photos would impact people for about five seconds then eventually end up in the recycling bin. The structures I built, on the other hand, would be a part of people's lives for years. There was also a feeling of satisfaction that was far more profound than shooting a great photo. So I bought a house with a big shop and started my company, OutsideUp in 2004. All structures are one-of-a-kind and custom-built to my client's specifications. Most are corrugated steel buildings with one cedar-shingled shed thrown in. I use a variety of reclaimed materials like doors, windows and siding, and there's examples of each among these buildings. I build the steel sliding doors and the slatted wood doors myself, and often add cedar trim, beams or rafters for style.

"I've been a handyman since I can remember. I gained the skills to build from my dad who could always devise a solution to any problem. My favorite was the clever hitch he built to tow a second lawn mower behind his big rider so he could cut even more grass in less time. Later, among my many jobs, I apprenticed with a terrific carpenter for a few years. He taught me the finer skills, but more importantly, a close attention to detail."

"I get a lot of repeat business from satisfied clients. Most of my new business comes through the website from both search and online advertising. I also get a fair number of referrals, and I often meet people who introduce themselves when I'm working in their neighbor's front yard."

CHAPTER TWO

Planning From The Ground Up

Location, Location, Location

The common wisdom about real estate — it's all about the location — applies equally to sheds. Even the coolest outbuilding, if it is inconveniently placed, won't maximize its potential or integrate itself optimally into the overall landscape. If you have a choice, it is worth taking some time to think about the best place to put your shed: do you want it to feel like a small oasis that is gradually "discovered" as one roams across the property, or do you imagine that it will be a visual focal point that immediately stands out? The potential use of the shed may inspire part of this choice: a home office where you imagine meeting with clients may be best situated near the main entrance to a property; this will help to quickly orient visitors and guide them forward. A private retreat for yoga or meditation, on the other hand, may not need to advertise itself as boldly, and setting it off the beaten path may help to establish the emotional tone for the experiences that it will offer.

Siting

Depending on the size and configuration of your yard, you may not have a lot of choice in how you situate your shed —your hand may be forced by a lack of space, for example, or you might have trees or other plantings that more or less dictate the shed's placement. In other situations, however, you might have some latitude in your decision-making process. In this case, here is a list of factors that you might want to consider:

Sunlight

You may wish to orient your shed so that you can place windows or doors on its south side: this will provide the most natural lighting during the day, which will not only save money on lighting — and heating on cooler days — but it may help to enhance the interior ambience. Conversely, if you live in a hot, sunny place, you may want to omit window's on the south side to keep the temperature down.

Shade

Are there any trees or large structures that cast shadows on the yard? If so, you may want to think about building the shed in a spot that takes advantage of the shade to help keep the interior cool in the summer.

Traffic flow & layout

Larger yards in particular can benefit from considering the overall traffic flow from one part of the yard to another. This factor applies to the way the yard is currently set up, but if you're planning on making other changes to the lot, now is the time to try and anticipate how it might all work together.

Access from the house

Do you imagine that you'll be moving directly from the house to the shed fairly often, or will you mostly access the shed from a location in the yard? The shed at our house — the writer's workshop — features doors on two sides to allow for the best possible access.

Types and sizes of doors & windows

My writer's workshop has a small, 32"-wide door on one end so that our family can enter on one end of the shed, but the other end of the shed features a large set of double doors that provide light and air in abundance. Even if it is chilly outside, these doors have large glass panes that help the interior to feel more visual connected with the rest of the yard. This simple trick also helps the interior to feel larger than it is by extending the site lines and "borrowing" space from beyond its walls.

Ancillary structures

Adding a deck, pergola, or arbor is an inexpensive way of increasing the usable "footprint" of your shed. By visually "annexing" the surrounding space, a shed can be transformed into a much more useful and appealing place to spend time. I've seen nice little porches added onto sheds to create covered seating areas, for example. And if you're expanding the area, you'll want to start from the ground up. That's why most shed conversations eventually turn to the topic of foundations. You'll want to understand the options before you proceed. Sheds are basically built in two ways: on-grade, or with frost-proof below-grade reinforcements. The first category is by far the most common, because you're simply building directly on the ground using beefy pressure-treated lumber, pre-cast concrete "spot" footings, or concrete blocks (see photo below). You then construct the walls on top of these components. For most sheds in most places, this method is adequate, and you'll see it used throughout this book.

The second and far less common solution is to dig down into the ground and pour large concrete footings. This approach essentially mimics the process used in building houses and other large permanent structures, and it is often considered to be overkill for sheds.

Pre-cast spot footings can provide a simple and inexpensive foundation for a shed. Their tops feature recesses that allow you to run dimensional lumber (2x4's, 2x6's or 2x8's) from one block to another, and this method makes it easy to create a level floor — simply dig down beneath any footing that are too high, or add clean fill below a footing that sits too low. Because they sit about 8-10" above the ground, you'll have to step up into the shed. This may not make a difference, but it is something to be aware of.

With all of this taken into account, many people opt for an on-grade approach that also offers a beefy and durable floor at a pretty reasonable expense: they pour a concrete slab. This offers a solid floor and provides a sturdy surface to which the walls can be attached. Constructing the slab can be hired out, if you like, or if you're inclined, you can rent a concrete mixer and handle the job yourself. I have a fair bit of experience in these matters, and I like to use a hybrid approach: I build the forms, and then pay a concrete truck to deliver ready-mixed concrete that they pour in place. This way, I only spend an hour or two, total, and minimize the heavy lifting. The cost usually runs about $300 for an 8' x10' slab, poured 3" thick. If you buy bagged concrete mix, an area this size can run you nearly $200. For me, that extra hundred dollars is very well spent.

Pouring a Concrete Slab

You will generally want to prep the area prior to pouring concrete — at a minimum, this means, ensuring that the spot is flat, level and free of debris. If you want to go the extra mile, you may wish to lay down a bed of gravel first, which will allow for good drainage of water from below the slab as well as providing a

To hold up over time, a concrete slab really needs to be reinforced. This is easily accomplished by placing metal grids called remesh inside the forms. The concrete will flow around the metal and, once it cures, the metal will help to keep the concrete from cracking later on. Remesh is inexpensive — around $8 for a 4' x 7' piece — and you can also purchase it in large rolls and just cut off the lengths that you need. You'll want to make sure to lift the remesh up so that it doesn't sit directly on the ground — it should be approximately centered in the middle of the forms.

firm foundation for the concrete.

Building forms is easy and instructive — forms that are truly level will show you any discrepancies in the building site itself. Sometimes, even pieces of ground that look flat aren't, and you might notice one or more low spots that need to be filled in so that you don't waste concrete.

For sheds, forms usually involve inexpensive 2x4's that are screwed or nailed together into a rectangle, such as on the concrete pad shown at top, left. To keep them from moving around during the pour, you may wish to secure the forms by pounding in stakes around the perimeter. Beware, however, that once they've been used for forms, lumber isn't usually good for much else, so most forming materials are often somewhat "sacrificial" by nature.

Things To Think About Before You Pour

- If you're planning to run power to the shed, you have the option of bringing it up through the slab, as shown in the opening photo. The ABS pipe that you see in the slab was installed as a "chase" through which wires can be fed when the time is right.

- Putting in a drain, depending on the use. For example, I have a plan to build a small shed for a pottery studio. It won't need to be large, but a floor drain would help with cleanup, so I'll be sure to integrate this feature when I pour a slab.

- How will you finish the concrete? You can leave it as is, or trowel it smooth, or you can stamp it when it is still wet to provide a more refined look (as shown here). Stamps can be rented at concrete suppliers nationwide and are an easy and inexpensive way to create the look of stone, tile, or brick. If you apply a stain after the concrete has cured, the effect can be quite striking.

Attaching the shed walls to the slab is easily done with "J" bolts that are set into the wet concrete. This isn't the only option, however (see illustration at right). I once built a shed on a pre-existing slab where no "J" bolts were present, so we anchored the walls by drilling through the bottom plate (the horizontal 2x4 that rests on the slab) and setting anchors into the concrete. This method will probably require a hammer drill, or at the very least, a powerful drill with a masonry bit. It takes more time and effort, but the end result is good.

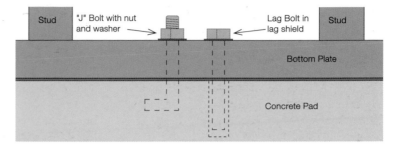

Attaching wooden framing to a concrete slab usually requires the use of "J" bolts or lags. This is pretty straight-forward, but you'll want to make sure to use pressure-treated material for the bottom plate, as this spot could be prone to collecting moisture and you'll want to make sure that you don't have any problems with rot down the road.

Flooring Options

If you're not up for pouring a concrete slab, fear not, lots of great sheds have options:

- Wood (simple plywood)
- Plain old dirt
- Brick or pavers

Whether your floor is ultimately made from concrete, plywood, or lumber, it can be dressed up with just about any kind of finished flooring (carpeting, wood, or tile) depending on the look and functional attributes that you have in mind. People often worry that this might break the budget, but you have to remember that you're talking about a pretty small amount of space. Even if you fancy a high-end flooring product, the small size of the building might mean that you'll only need a small quantity, which can help to keep the overall costs reasonable. It is also worth pointing out that it can be easy to find small quantities of a given style of flooring sold at closeout prices: these quantities are often too small for a large room in a house, but they might be sufficient enough to outfit a shed.

A tile floor can be laid down on a concrete slab or a wooden floor that has a layer of backer-board screwed to it. Tile floors are nice because they're so durable and easy to clean, and small quantities of tile can often be purchased at bargain prices.

Wood strip flooring looks great and is fairly easy to install — you could go with solid wood, or engineered flooring. In any event, make sure to follow the manufacturer's instructions regarding proper installation of a vapor barrier — especially if you're installing on top of a concrete slab.

Brick flooring is one of my favorites for creating a rustic ambience, but it can be expensive if you're purchasing new bricks. This might be a great place to re-purpose some old bricks if you can get your hands on them.

These modular carpet tiles go down quickly and can be arranged however you like to create a pattern of your own choosing. Available in a variety of colors and styles, they are reasonably priced and can be replaced individually if one becomes ruined. They're fastened together with small self-adhesive stickers on their undersides and you can create area rugs, runners, or wall-to-wall carpeting, as you wish.

Technicalities

When I talk to people about building a shed, I am invariably asked the same questions every time, and for good reason:

What kinds of restrictions and regulations apply to a shed?

Will we need to apply for a permit? Is that a hassle? Is it expensive?

Will we have to deal with a building inspector?

The answers to all of these questions are generally positive — meaning that building a shed isn't a major project and that it can be executed with a minimum of administrative work. Fortunately, most municipalities follow a provision in the International Building Code (IBC) which stipulates that small accessory buildings (sheds) under 120 square feet (10'x12', or any other comparable proportion) are exempt from a building permit. This means that you will not incur additional fees or have to work with a building inspector. However, you will still want to be aware of any potential zoning requirements. This will generally govern the placement of a shed relative to property lines, although local rules may vary. In a country this large, there are always bound to be exceptions. In Portland, Oregon, for example a shed must be under 200sf to be exempt from a building permit, but a zoning permit is required.

Before undertaking any construction project such as this, it is a good idea to check the ordinances in your area, since running afoul of local building codes can be a recipe for disaster. Most of this information can easily be found online — just head to the website of your municipality and check out the related pages. It is also worth noting that some areas may have special restrictions. In our area, certain neighborhoods are designated as historic districts, and this brings with it some regulations that go above and beyond other neighborhoods in the city.

Develop a budget

Budgeting for a project of this scale isn't much different than anything else — you might already have a "bottom line" amount in mind in terms of what you can spend, but do you know exactly what you'll be spending your money on and how much it'll run you? This budgeting worksheet might help you to get a handle on your potential costs and identify any trouble spots early on. If you're really lucky, you might find that the whole thing comes in below your target figure. Either way, it is important to figure out how much you'll need to budget and what it is going for. It is easier to make adjustments to the overall project's scope or particulars before the actual construction process is set into motion.

This worksheet is designed to help you compare the cost of different options so that you can see how best to proceed. I allowed for three different design variations (cleverly named options 1-3), and by varying the materials you use, you can lay out shed designs at a number of different price points. By having all of the information on one page, you'll be able to make decisions as you go forward. Not all of the categories may seem relevant to your project, so just ignore them if this is the case. To be as comprehensive as I could, I put a few extra lines at the end labeled "other" so that you'll have a place to add on if need be.

SHED BUDGETING WORKSHEET

	OPTION 1	OPTION 2	OPTION 3
Foundation (concrete)			
Foundation (wood deck)			
Dirt floor			
Wall & roof framing & sheathing			
Siding: wooden clapboards			
Siding: T-111 4x8 panels			
Siding: cedar shakes			
Siding: other			
Roofing: asphalt shingles			
Roofing: cedar shakes			
Roofing: galvanized tin			
Roofing: other			
Doors: prefab, double set			
Doors: prefab, single			
Doors: DIY, double			
Doors: DIY, single			
Windows: new, operable			
Windows: new, fixed			
Windows: salvaged			
Windows: DIY made			
Cabinetry/storage: prefab			
Cabinetry/storage: salvaged			
Cabinetry/storage:DIY made			
Cabinetry/storage: other			
Fancy trim: materials			
Fancy trim: DIY labor			
Fancy trim: paid labor			
Electric hookup/wiring			
Other			
Other			
Other			
Other			
Other			
Other			
TOTAL			

CHAPTER THREE
Gear Girl

Jo Varner is definitely an exemplar of the classic scholar/athlete archetype. During the day, she is completing a PhD at the University of Utah where she studies pikas, but in her free time, she can usually be found in the mountains near her home. Two of her favorite outdoor pursuits are downhill skiing and mountain biking, both of which are pretty gear-intensive. This means that she has accumulated quite a lot of biking and skiing equipment, and she needed a dedicated place to store it so that she could reclaim her living room. Jo also does all of her own maintenance, which means that she waxes her skis and tunes her bikes on a regular basis, and she hoped that a small shed would give her the workshop space that she really needed for both of these tasks. We put our heads together and came up with a design that is working out great for her. The final design is both practical and attractive.

Materials Spotlight: Reclaimed lumber

Jo had the good fortune of tackling the shed project at the same time that her parents, who also live in town, were replacing a huge deck. This meant that she was on the receiving end of a van load of used redwood 2x4's, all of which were weathered but fundamentally sound. She was able to reuse this material and score on a couple of fronts: she saved about $220 on lumber, and she created a good home for a ton (almost literally) of perfectly use-able material.

On the following pages are step-by-step photos that should be useful for aspiring shed builders. They show the actual steps involved in the construction.

The location for the shed was fairly well dictated by the layout of the yard — a large empty spot near the back door of the house seemed like the obvious place. Beyond that, we had a list of things that we wanted to use, had on hand or wanted to include:

- Sliding door
- Window for interior light
- Simple shed roof to maximize the ceiling height throughout the entire interior
- Galvanized material
- Bike rack to use wall space to store bikes
- Workbench for ski waxing and bike tunes
- A bike repair stand that can be carried out front
- Ski chair
- Ski rack located in the space between the door and window opening
- Overhead shelving & cabinet space
- A couple of framed posters commemorating Jo's love of the mountains

1 The shed's future home was the perfect size, and the spot was nice and level, which saved us work. An out-of-level spot will either need to be flattened out or built up in some way to provide a good base for the floor.

2 Shed floors can be built in a couple of different ways. Wood floors are usually constructed more or less like this: you build a frame with the 2x4's set on edge, making sure to space the infill 2x4's (those in the center of the frame) at 16" centers. This ensures that the floor will be rigid when the subflooring is attached.

3 To avoid having a big step up into the shed, it is nice to keep the frame as close to the ground as possible. The frame can be raised off the ground, however, and there are generally two reasons to do this. For one thing, you may wish to elevate the frame to keep it away from moisture, or you might need to "shim" it slightly to get it exactly level (as was the case here). In either case, you'll need to properly support every part of the frame — failure to do so will result in a floor that moves around underfoot. Concrete pavers are commonly used for this purpose, as they are inexpensive and easy to work with.

4 In a small building like this, it is pretty easy to build the entire frame and then check it all around with a level to see how it sits. Any low spots can be built up with pavers, or high spots can be dug away with a spade.

5 For a building to end up square, it has to begin that way. This makes a difference because a discrepancy early on will follow you all the way through the process. An out-of-square floor means that the roof overhangs won't be even, for example, and this error will be pretty noticeable in the finished product. The best way to square an object of this size is by measuring the diagonals and making adjustments to the frame until the measurements are equal to within a 1/16". By the way, this method works great on smaller stuff too, like cabinet doors, drawers, or just about anything else for that matter.

6 Once the frame has been squared, you'll want to put on the subflooring. To get a really rigid floor, the nailing schedule is important. Place 16D nails 6" apart along the outside edge of the frame and 12" apart in the center. If this sounds like a lot of nails, it is — that's the point. I use a cordless framing nailer for this, which I love, since I don't care for the noise and weight of compressors. If this method doesn't work for you, I recommend renting a nailer for the day — it'll save a lot of time. That said, the old fashioned method (aka a hammer) works fine too if you're not in a rush.

7 Any time that you're fastening panels to a framework made of studs, you need to make sure that the edges of the plywood land on the center of the studs. This will allow you to properly secure the plywood. Sometimes you'll get lucky and the studs will magically be in the right place, but other times you might need to rip the plywood down to size. In other cases, you might find that it is faster to just add another 2x4 to the frame.

8 A completed floor deck is invaluable as a place to assemble the walls. It is much easier to layout 2x4's on a flat surface than on a patch of grass. This picture shows the intersection of the top plate (the sloping 2x4 at the top of the wall) and the studs on the front and back of the wall. My method for laying out walls like this — especially in this case where I'm not working from an exact set of plans — is to lay out the parts so that they look right, and then mark the cuts from there. I don't worry about figuring out what angles to cut the studs to: I am experienced enough to trust that I can just swing the blade on the miter saw so that it matches the cut line. This approach may not be appropriate for fine interior finish carpentry, but for rough work like framing, it always works.

9 Sheathing the walls is also much easier on the deck than after the walls have gone up. The nailing schedule is the same as for the floors: 12" in the field (center of the panel) and 6" on the edges.

11 The rear wall is constructed in the same way.

10 A completed wall of this size is easy to stand up, even if you're working alone. To keep it in place, just nail a couple of diagonal braces in place. They'll be removed later once there are more walls in place.

12 With two walls in place, the shed is starting to take shape. The two walls can be nailed together with 16d nails at 6" intervals.

13 The framing goes quickly on a project of this size. Even working alone, I had the walls up in less than a couple of hours. It is pretty satisfying work.

14 To get started on the front wall, I actually built it in place. This made it easier to visualize where the window and door openings would fall and ensure that they were the right size. Again, since I didn't have plans drawn out for this shed, I could employ a bit of a "design as you go". I also had the flexibility of knowing that I would be building the doors and windows, so the rough openings really didn't have to conform to any particular dimensions.

15 Although it is easier to apply sheathing to walls prior to lifting them up, it isn't too big a deal to tack on a panel vertically when necessary.

16 Here's my trick for sheathing existing walls when you're working alone: put a couple of screws (or nails) in between the subfloor and the bottom plate. They will hold the sheathing in the right spot for you, which makes for a relatively stress-free procedure.

17 As the wall framing began to take shape, I began to think about the roof. I spaced the rafters on 24" centers.

18 Just like when you're putting on sheathing, it is important that the edges of the roofing panels are properly supported. In this case, that pretty much took care of itself: the roof was 8' wide, and it was made of panels with seams every 24", so the rafters just happened to be in the right places.

19 While I didn't have to cut any of the tin for width (you almost never do — you can just overlap it more or less to get the width to work out), I did need to trim it to length. Tin snips are a fast and easy way of doing this. You could also use an angle grinder with a thin cutting blade, or a jigsaw with a blade designed for cutting metal. I like the snips because they're quiet, and they're almost as fast.

20 Jo and I came up with a design that features a small overhanging roof at the front of this shed. We imagined that it would create a nice shady spot to set up a bike repair stand on hot summer days. To determine the size and pitch of the roof, I experimented with some 2x4's until I got it to look right. The overhang extended 4', because I used the offcuts from 12' roofing panels that I trimmed down to 8' for the larger portion of the roof.

21 The front edge of the roof was supported by a pair of 4x4 posts. To keep the posts from sinking into the ground, I used pre-cast concrete blocks that are designed for this purpose (they're also great for supporting a shed floor if you don't mind the added height). To hold the 4x4 in place, I tacked on a brace from scrap OSB.

22 Setting up the supports for the overhang was tricky, since I didn't have an assistant, but it shaped up quickly enough. The span between the posts (just shy of 8') didn't seem large enough to require an additional center post, and keeping the space open was definitely a priority.

23 The back edge of the small roof was screwed to a 2x4 cleat that ran across the front of the shed.

24 We got really resourceful when it came to trimming out this shed: I had enough 2x4's left after construction to allow me to rip a bunch of them in half and send them through my planer. The result? ¾" trim stock that showed off the natural color of the redwood.

25 An angle finder, used in conjunction with a level, made it a snap to determine the cutting angle for the vertical trim pieces, where they met the roof.

26 I got a screaming deal on a pile of ¼" hickory plywood, so I decided to use it as siding for the shed. This pretty panel would usually be cut up for kitchen cabinet doors, or something along those lines, so it was fun to use it in a different setting. As long as it is stained and maintained, it will hold up fine outdoors.

27 Jo brought up the idea of a sliding door mounted on some beefy hardware, and I loved the idea. This track is part of the same system that is used on barns, and it is really beefy. The installation process begins by mounting the track above the door opening. Use a level to make sure that it is properly aligned.

28 The system is really simple: there are two little wheeled carriages that roll around inside the track. They each feature a bolt that hangs downward, and the door is simply fastened to the bolt. This will make sense in the photos to come.

29 The door begins as a simple rectangular frame. I used 2x4's to make it nice and sturdy.

30 After I drilled a pair of holes in the horizontal piece at the top of the door frame, I inserted the bolts through the holes and then threaded on the nuts and washers. The door's height can be adjusted by moving the nuts up or down. This also allows you to adjust the door and make it plumb and level. It is a really simple system, but it works great. The exact location of the holes that you drill isn't critical, either — just be sure to put one near each edge of the door and you can't go wrong.

31 I covered the door frame with a ¼" panel made from hickory plywood

32 For looks, I trimmed out the door panel with a frame and "X" braces.

33 I couldn't find a stock handle that I really loved, so I made one from a 15" length of 1" dowel and some hardware I had on hand. Getting the scale right made a difference, at least in my mind.

34 The shed has one tall, skinny window which I trimmed out with redwood that I ripped down from the original pile of 2x4's. For security reasons, the window is narrow enough to keep intruders out.

This simple ski rack was made from a scrap 2x4 and some 6" lengths of PVC pipe. It helps keep the skis out of the way yet still close at hand.

This bench is where Jo will be able to set up her equipment to tune her skis once the snow flies. It has plenty of storage space below, and the framed posters will provide some inspiration.

A bike rack like this frees up floor space so you can move around, and it was easy to build with scraps left over from the shed construction. I used a couple of 12"-long pieces of pipe insulation to cover the top edge of the "arms" and keep the bike frame from getting scratched.

When the weather permits, Jo can do her bike repairs outside, thanks to this handy homemade bike stand. The awning provides some shade on hot summer days.

The perfect finishing touch: an Adirondack chair dressed up with old skis.

GALLERY

(LEFT) The bold purple paint and the unusual rooflines make this into an eye-catcher. (ABOVE) This shed is butted directly up to a low deck so that it forms a nice backdrop and creates the feeling of an outdoor room.

(LEFT) The clapboard siding and oversized hinges on this little guy add a lot of charm. (ABOVE) This beautiful shed was just completed and is going to be turned into a pottery studio. The owner has been taking pottery classes for years at a studio in town, and finally decided to take the plunge and create her own dream studio right outside her back door. The transom window lets in a lot of light, and the paint and trim details tie in nicely with her home.

Photo Courtesy of Elliott Brown

This shed has so much going for it: the Tudor-style exposed beams that punctuate the exterior planes, the clusters of pegs that protrude from the joints of said beams, and the eye-catching green doors. The steep pitch of the roof is a pretty dramatic element, too.

With its cedar roof and traditional detailing — plus the fact that it is set amidst lavender plants in full flower — this looks like a pretty quaint garden shed. But all the ventilation would probably make it comfortable to use for much more than that, even in the height of summer.

Photo Courtesy of Elliott Brown

CHAPTER FOUR

Writer's Retreat

This shed began as a pretty ordinary outbuilding that provided little more than a place to store bikes, holiday decorations, and whatever else didn't quite fit into the house. This worked out fine — frankly we were just happy to have the extra storage space — but I always had the feeling that it wasn't living up to its full potential. Eventually, I realized that it could be transformed into the home office that I'd been craving for a while. Even better, I figured that, by doing the work myself, I could do it on the cheap, and still end up with a pretty satisfying space that would look great.

Here's the background: I have been writing professionally for nearly a decade, but have never had a proper office to do it in. Our home works for our family, for the most part, but we don't have the luxury of unused rooms where I could set up a desk, bookcases and the kind of large corkboard that would help me to stay organized. Laptop computers do make it easy to work anyplace in the house, and there is a certain convenience to that, but frankly, I got pretty fed up with this nomadic working style. The dining room table kind of worked, as did a corner of the kitchen counter, but every time I wanted to sit down to write, I needed to spread out a heap of books, notes, and drawings, and the whole mess had to be picked up when I was done. This made the process kind of annoying, and it also cre-

ated an uncomfortable rootless feeling. My writing brings in some extra money, and I really enjoy it, to boot — why shouldn't I have a dedicated space to do it in? The solution ultimately came from taking a good look at our backyard shed and coming up with cre-

ative ways to store its contents and also do a simple remodel that would turn it into a pleasant office space.

I had a few challenges that I'm guessing aren't unique to our situation, and I came up

PLANNING:
List-Making 101

I realize that not everyone works this way, but I'm the kind of guy who makes a lot of lists, and time and experience have proven that it is the best way for me to get my ideas organized. If this resonates with you, then keep reading. I find that a project like this can get off to a good start by making not one but two kinds of lists: things you'll need, and things you don't need. While the second category may seem unnecessary, I think that it goes a long way toward defining how the project will proceed. Here are the lists that I made as I planned out my writer's retreat:

What I needed:

- A small couch — nothing too big or deep, and nothing fancy. A lot of my work involves reading and researching, and it is nice to be able to lay back while doing so.
- A desk. The bigger the better.
- Bookcases. Like, a whole wall full.
- A decent desk chair. Nothing fancy, just something that swivels
- A rug, preferably a faded and slightly shabby oriental rug that could get dirty and not look worse for it.
- Electricity for a printer, laptop, etc.
- A small space heater for wintertime use.
- Corkboards. A lot. Like 4' x 6' or bigger.
- WiFi. This was already in place — our yard already has great reception from our wireless system.

What I didn't need:

- A phone line. My wife and I haven't had a land-line in nearly a decade, and don't miss it. Cell phones work great for us.
- A TV.
- A conference or meeting table. The office isn't a place that I planned to meet clients (I own a woodworking studio ten minutes away where I meet with clients). The office is just for me.
- A bathroom or kitchenette. The office is located ten steps from our house, which has all the plumbing I need.
- A lot of drawers for storage.
- File storage.

with some pretty good solutions. One of the main concerns — especially on the part of my wife — was where we'd put the stuff that already lived in the shed. This wasn't a trivial question, but fortunately, I'm an optimist, and I knew we'd come up with something. After giving it some thought (ok, a lot of thought, and a few conversations where I desperately pleaded my case with my ever-patient spouse), I came up with two strategies. Fortunately, the shed features fairly high ceilings. The side walls are 8' high, and the ceilings, at their peak, are almost 10' from the floor. I reasoned that I could use some of this space to create a couple of storage nooks that would be out of the way but still have a pretty large capacity. When I didn't need to get into the nooks, they could be covered up by draping some fabric to hide the clutter. This worked out great, especially after undertaking a ruthless love-it-or-lose-it cleaning session which helped us winnow out a lot of junk that we were hoarding for no good reason.

We did have some stuff that was too big for the nooks, however, and we needed another solution. Our bikes were the single biggest objects in the shed, and we use them just about every day, so ready access wasn't negotiable. We actually have a lot of bikes — six between my wife and I, plus a trailer for our young daughter — and so I came up with a compromise strategy. A couple of the bikes could be stored in the shed — they do look pretty nice, after all — and the others (along with things like our lawnmower and rakes) would be relegated to a small auxiliary structure that we playfully termed "the Shannex", which is our shorthand for shed annex. Since we had a small, unused area between the shed and the fence at the edge of our property, I enclosed this space with wall and a roof and put in a door to access it via the shed. This solution satisfied everyone: it was quick, cheap, and practical. My wife still had easy access to the things that needed to be stored out there, and I got to have a relatively clutter-free workspace.

While this concept may not work for everybody, I've seen variations on this theme save the day a couple of times. I know plenty of people who use a relatively large shed to hold just a few essential items that don't really need to take up the volume of space that they do. Perhaps constructing a tiny "storage only" shed for garden tools would free up the main shed for a more creative use? It is something worth considering.

Planning tip: The one paragraph summary.

If you're working with other people on this project, it might be handy to have a quick, easy summary of the project that captures the highlights of what you're trying to do. Is this essential? Maybe not, but it can't hurt, and besides, I've found that it always helps me to clarify my own vision when I write it out. Here's an example:

I'd like a comfortable and efficient office that I can use as a home-base for my writing career. I would like plenty of shelf space for books and magazines. I'd also like to have a lot of display area where I can pin up photos, articles, and other snippets that relate to my projects. The space should be bright (i.e. drywalled and painted off-white), but not overly stark. I also want it to feel like a dedicated office space, and not like I simply put a computer in a room filled with rakes, shovels, and the occasional bag of potting soil. If I have to store some non-office stuff there, I want to have those things concealed behind doors or in cabinets.

The Process, Step-by-Step

So that explains the story behind the shed, and how I planned it out. How did I actually go about the transformation? This next segment provides an in-depth look at the details, and it also shows the overall sequence that I worked in.

What did it cost?

Structurally, the shed was in great shape. I built it from the ground up about five years ago, at a cost of around $900, and it didn't require any maintenance or repair work. That meant that I could put my money into the finishes (i.e. the aspects of the project that contribute to its look and feel). I figured it would cost around $500, and through a combination of creativity and thriftiness, it came in just under that amount. Here's where the money went:

$140 drywall and joint compound

$55 wall & trim paint

$95 electrical supplies

$30 plywood for the overhead storage nooks

$10 couch (thank God for yard sales)

$18 bookcase materials

$37 turned legs for the desk

$62 plexiglas for the door panels

$32 curtains & rods

$12 flooring adhesive

$491

I also saved money by making all the interior window trim and baseboards from scraps that I had on hand.

1 This picture shows how bad things had gotten prior to the remodel — the shed was plenty big, but completely unorganized. We basically just heaped stuff against the walls and tried to keep some space clear in the middle so that we could get bikes in and out. Oh, the shame of it all.

3 A major key to the success of this project was our ability to annex a small nook on the other side of the shed so that we could turn it into some extra storage space. I planned to access it via a new door from the inside of the shed. I cut out the opening with a sawzall, and reinforced it with 2x4's as needed.

2 Once the clutter was removed, I began to see that we had a lot of space to work with and I could start to imagine how things might shape up.

4 For the shed to function as an office, I knew I would need some outlets. It was really easy to put them in since the stud walls were still exposed. I used non-metallic outlet boxes that are designed for new construction — they just fasten directly to the studs.

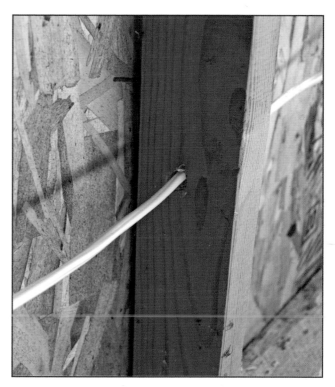

5 By drilling through the center of the studs, I could ensure that the romex would be unlikely to be hit by screws from both the inside and outside of the building.

6 With the rough electrical in place, I went ahead with the drywall. The first step was measuring the locations of the outlets so that I could lay them out on the drywall sheet. The first question to answer is how far from the ground the outlet is located.

7 It is also necessary to measure the placement of each outlet from the spot where the edge of the drywall will be placed.

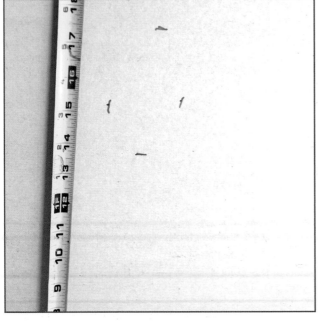

8 These measurements can be transferred to the drywall. These marks indicate the edges of the outlet cutout.

9 With the cutout completed, it is time to hoist the sheet into place.

10 A drywall saw is usually the best tool to remove material around window and door edges.

11 This wall was the most time-consuming, because it had two outlets, two windows, and a doorway to work around.

12 I covered the seams with self-adhesive mesh tape in preparation for joint compound. Here's a quick tip — don't put up more tape than you're planning to cover up at a given time. It will begin to droop or even fall off after a while if you don't get some mud on there. Ceilings are particularly troublesome in this regard.

13 I am hardly a pro when it comes to slinging mud, but I've done quite a bit of it, so I've found that the style that works for me is to apply more thin coats rather than fewer thick ones. I don't mind doing four coats because I can apply each one very quickly, and I take great care to not apply too much joint compound at a given time. The worst mistake I've made in the past is to mud too heavily, and then the sanding takes longer and is far messier. I'd rather sneak up on a good result with thin coats and avoid the mess and tedium.

14 To mud the obtuse angle between the walls and ceiling, I used heavy duty scissors to trim a piece of plastic to fit the required profile. This approach worked out great.

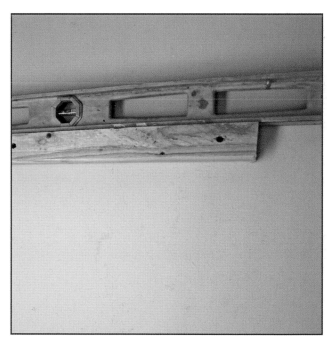

15 This shed has fairly tall ceilings: the side walls are eight feet high, and it is ten feet tall at the peak. I decided to install a couple of storage platforms overhead to take advantage of the height. The platforms consisted of ¾" CDX plywood that was supported by 2x2's secured to the studs with 4" screws.

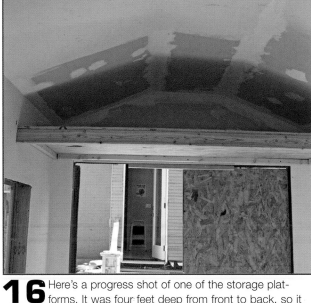

16 Here's a progress shot of one of the storage platforms. It was four feet deep from front to back, so it held quite a bit of stuff.

17 To keep the shed feeling open, I decided to build a simple desk that was supported by turned legs, rather than a bulkier piece of furniture with integral cabinets that would visually hog up space.

18 The furnishings that I built for this office were uber-simple: just ¾" plywood boxes outfitted with shelves as needed. This wall cabinet provided much-needed storage above the desk, and I tried to create a composed look by painting all of the pieces the same color.

19 When it came time to trim out the interior, I found that it was easiest to just set up a small tablesaw and a couple of saw horses on the adjacent deck. This way I could trim casings and moldings to size as necessary.

20 The shed has three windows, all of varying sizes, and I decided to trim them all out in eclectic, non-matching styles that were all inspired by Victorian motifs that are common in our neighborhood. I decided that the easiest way to get a good result was to build a complete unit for each window, and then I attach the units inside with construction adhesive and nails. By painting the units prior to installation, I avoided the need to mask off the surrounding drywall — this saved a ton of time and effort. I like to pre-finish wood trim in this manner whenever possible. I find that it creates a better result and there's no downside to it.

21 The completed window trim units were quick to build and paint, and they went a long way toward helping the interior feel finished.

22 I actually like the rough concrete floor of the shed, but I knew that I wanted something slightly more refined to dress it up. At first I figured I'd look for a shabby-chic area rug at local antique stores, but then I remembered that I had a stack of leftover Armstrong vinyl tiles from a project about five years ago. The colors were pretty much what I'd had in mind, as luck would have it. By adhering the tiles to the concrete with a manufacturer-recommended adhesive, I created a nice focal point for the room and also made a smooth surface for a wheeled office chair to roll around on.

Running electricity to an outbuilding

This is one of the most useful upgrades that you can undertake, and it can usually be done fairly quickly and at a pretty reasonable cost. As with any project involving electricity, make sure to check with your local building codes to make sure that you are in compliance. When in doubt, leave the project to a licensed electrician. You may consider a hybrid approach, as I did here: certain aspects of this kind of project are well within the reach of a capable homeowner, and you can just call in the pros when you need to. I did all of the safe, easy work, such as digging the trench and running the wires through the flexible conduit. I made the connections along the circuit at the outlet boxes and at the outdoor circuit box where the wires joined the romex on the building's interior. I am very experienced with this kind of work and am comfortable with it. For safety's sake, I hired an electrician to connect the new circuit to the electrical panel inside the house. This strategy saved money, and I got the satisfaction of doing as much of the project as I could.

Before you get to the stage where you start putting in outlets, however, you'll want to determine the size of the loads that you'll have, and choose both the wire and breaker accordingly. I planned to run a light and two outlets to power a laptop computer and printer, which is a fairly light duty application. With this in mind, I planned for a 20-amp circuit and 12-gauge wire. If this part seems confusing, you can look online for help or consult with a pro. Having this decision made allowed me to run the romex inside the shed and then drywall up the open wall cavities.

The other main consideration is how to get the power from the source to the destination. Trenching is the most common solution, and this task will be rendered easier or harder depending simply on the amount of ground you

have to cover. I had to dig a trench about 14' long, so it only took about an hour. Really long hauls might justify renting a machine to do most of the dirty work. Weigh your options (factoring in stuff like the price of gas and how long it will take you to drive to the rental place and back) and you'll easily figure out which method is the best use of your time and money.

You have some options when it comes to deciding what kind of wire to use: the simplest and least expensive is called direct-bury cable, which is basically romex with a thicker skin. I was concerned, however, about the possibility of somebody (namely me) accidentally hitting it with a shovel in the future, as the cable was going to be placed near some garden beds, so I looked into a couple of other approaches. A fairly standard solution involves using lengths of rigid conduit, which is inexpensive, but it is more time-consuming to install. You'll need to spend a lot more time laying out the run, making cuts as needed and joining the segments with angled and straight connectors to fit the trench. This might be a great choice, though, if your run is primarily long and straight. Just be aware that not all types of conduit are meant to be buried, so make sure to get the right one.

In the end, I decided to use a flexible conduit that cost me $35 for 50', and I could've done it with rigid conduit for around $15, but avoiding the time and effort of cutting the rigid pieces to length, joining them, and waiting for adhesive to dry was worth $20 in my opinion. The convenience factor of the flexible conduit made it very easy to use: I used a single piece to run through the ground and then up the side of the shed.

Running the wires through the conduit wasn't too bad of a chore. I started at the top and fed them through until they came out on the other side.

With the wires in place, I simply connected them to the romex that fed the outlets. The connections are tucked away inside a small exterior-rated junction box.

23 One of my pet peeves is seeing cords, so I look for ways to hide them when I can. I had planned to set my printer/scanner unit on the shelf above the desk, and I was able to run its cord through the wall behind it. This can be a pretty easy job, as long as you are just running the cord vertically within the same stud bay. I drilled a 1" hole in the cabinet to get things rolling.

24 Usually, I would just drop a cord down through the upper hole and let gravity pull it down toward the lower hole, but this cord had a large transformer on the bottom end that required me to fish it the other way around. I took a stiff piece of wire (a coat hanger will work) and tied it to the end of the cord. By pushing the stiff wire up into the lower hole, I was able to pass it up until I could reach into the upper hole and fish it out. Once the wire had emerged from the top, I just kept pulling until the cord popped out.

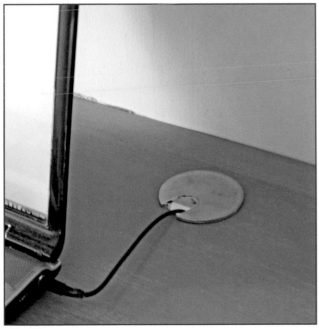

25 I also used a 2½" grommet for cord management on the desktop. I used a hole saw in my cordless drill.

26 Once the electricity had been run out to the shed (see the special section on this), I did the final electrical work, which consisted of wiring up a couple of outlets and testing them out.

27 With the interior of the shed mostly done, I needed to finish up the new bonus storage area that I planned to create in the small alley between the shed wall and the property's wooden fence. The spot was 12' long and 5' wide. This picture shows the area before I had cut the door in step 3.

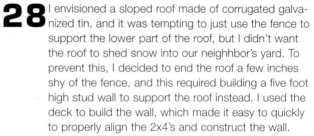

28 I envisioned a sloped roof made of corrugated galvanized tin, and it was tempting to just use the fence to support the lower part of the roof, but I didn't want the roof to shed snow into our neighhbor's yard. To prevent this, I decided to end the roof a few inches shy of the fence, and this required building a five foot high stud wall to support the roof instead. I used the deck to build the wall, which made it easy to quickly to properly align the 2x4's and construct the wall.

29 The wall simply paralleled the fence.

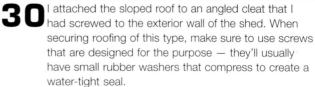

30 I attached the sloped roof to an angled cleat that I had screwed to the exterior wall of the shed. When securing roofing of this type, make sure to use screws that are designed for the purpose — they'll usually have small rubber washers that compress to create a water-tight seal.

This is just what I had in mind. The office is comfortable, or-derly, and it doesn't feel like a shed. I can now say that my favorite room in the house isn't actually in the house. The desk is the perfect size for the room and for my working habits. It doesn't dominate the space, but there is enough room to spread out comfortably. Having a small door on the one end makes for easy traffic flow, and it also provides a nice view from the desk. It also makes the surrounding space more interesting: by offering a glimpse into the shed, visitors are in-trigued and engaged with the space in a more interesting way.

Perhaps because I live in an old Victorian home, I have a penchant for fine interior woodworking. This one-of-a-kind window trim makes the statement that somebody cared enough to spend a few extra minutes. It also helps elevate the shed well beyond its utilitarian beginnings.

The couch was a great score at a yardsale a few blocks away, and the wall cabinets were left over from a remodeling job that I did a few years ago.

Storing a bike in the shed doesn't bother me a bit, since it is a nice-looking bike to begin with.

The large doors on the end open up completely, and this connects the shed quite nicely with the yard. There is plenty of fresh air and sunlight to be had, and because it offers such long sightlines, the interior feels much more spacious than it is.

GALLERY

I'm a sucker for a shed with a porch. You can also see that the plank siding has live edges, and the effect is beautiful. To find material like this, you'll have to drive right past the big box stores and find a sawmill. It may seem like a bit more work, but it'll be worth it: not only will you have some unique siding, but boards like these are often cheaper because less labor has gone into their production.

Who says that symmetry is essential? The side walls of this shed are different heights, and this raises design questions. Should the roof peak be centered or offset? How do you place the doors and windows on the front?

Rounded door and window openings are a bit more work if you're building them yourself, although they do add a lot of charm. Used building material stores might be a good source for unusual windows and doors at a great price.

Photos Courtesy of Henry Burrows

Cord wood has been used as infill on exterior walls for centuries — remains of such structures have been dated back over a thousand years. The technique is also called cordwood masonry, or stackwall construction. The walls can be as thin as 6", or as thick as a couple of feet. Cordwood construction often incorporates a timber frame construction to provide adequate load-bearing capacity for the walls and roof. Cordwood, by itself, may not be strong enough to create durable walls, although its strength certainly increases if you use thicker stock. The finished effect is striking, and small details like this bottle-glass window form a novel focal point.

It is easy to get into a rut and only build sheds that conform to a pretty toned-down, traditional aesthetic, but this design proves you don't have to: the wavy contour of the roof and the organic feel of the stucco show what is possible with a little creativity. The actual construction techniques aren't readily betrayed by the exterior, either — straw bale, maybe?

Photo Courtesy of Lara 604

CHAPTER FIVE

Recording Studio

Brit Merrill is a life-long musician whose current passion is playing clawhammer banjo in a couple of of bands in Salt Lake City, Utah. She has been a key member of the Bueno Avenue Stringband for about four years, and has more recently helped to found the Graveyard Chickens, another rootsy band that plays in the venerable old-time string band tradition (old time music is generally defined as the homegrown music that gave birth to bluegrass). Think fiddles & banjos on front porches and in back yards, and you'll get the idea. Both bands play pretty actively around town, including lots of weddings, square dances, and community events, and the latter band decided to take things up a notch and craft an album. This was a new venture for Brit, and she wasn't entirely sure how the process would unfold. As it turned out, she ended up with much more than she'd bargained for.

The goal for the album was primarily about creating a document for posterity, with very little focus on garnering fame or fortune. Because this kind of music usually only appeals to a real niche audience, the band members realized that their album

wasn't going to be a big money maker: there is an attitude in their musical community that boasts that "you can make literally dozens of dollars playing this stuff! But not all at once, of course. You have to be in it for the long haul." Knowing from the get-go that the project wasn't going to rake in the dough, they needed to keep it affordable. The solution was to take advantage of current technology and self-produce the album at home, as many other bands have been doing for a few years now.

As it happened, the desire to create an album dovetailed with an emerging recognition that the band really needed a better, more permanent practice space. Even though the band plays without amplifiers, they still make a lot of noise, and it was becoming harder and harder to schedule practice sessions that wouldn't inconvenience the other members of her household. Paying rent for an off-site space was both expensive and impractical, but Brit realized that a small backyard building might work out just right. It was right around this time that Brit asked me for my input, and I was eager to help out.

Developing a vision for the studio

The design process for any outbuilding can be fairly dynamic, and it certainly was in this case, too. One of the major considerations for planning is how to situate the shed on the property, and in this case, the decision was easy because a 9' x 9' concrete pad had been poured prior to Brit's purchase of the property. The pad was conveniently located near the back door of their home, so it was easy to zip back and forth to the kitchen or bathroom. When Brit purchased the property about five years ago, it came with a tiny plastic storage shed that was situated on the pad — this shed was simply moved to another spot so that it could continue its duty as a place to put gardening tools and the like (shown at left).

There was also an electrical outlet nearby on the side of the house (below left), so this made it convenient to simply run a short extension cord to the shed when electricity would be required. Not wiring the shed saved a fair bit of time and effort, but because the interior walls are open, it could be wired later on.

One unusual factor in the siting of this shed is the presence of an air conditioning unit between the shed and the house (below). Ideally, it would have been positioned closer to the fence, but that decision had already been made a long time ago, and it resulted in there being a small corner of the yard that was still useable, but tough to access without having to climb over the air conditioner. We remedied this problem by putting a door in the shed. Brit envisions using the

shed needed in terms of functionality. Because Brit's band plays acoustic music, they don't need a lot of equipment, and today's technology means that amateur musicians can self-produce CD's of respectable quality for very little money. With little more than a laptop computer and a good microphone, they could meet their goals pretty easily. Brit figured that they would need a simple desk to hold a computer that would run the recording software and provide a place to do the digital editing (below).

spot to store firewood for the occasional backyard bonfire.

Another oddball consideration with this site was that the pad was positioned below the adjacent deck, and this made us scratch our heads for a while. We wanted the main entrance to the shed (as well as its most adorned side) to face out toward the deck. The reason for this was mostly practical: it just made sense to place the entrance close to the back door of the house, so that you wouldn't have to walk all the way around the shed to gain entry. The difficulty came in contemplating how the door would function: if the door swung outward, it would bump into the elevated deck. We solved this problem by building a short walkway as an extension of the deck, and raising the bottom of the door to this height. This allowed the door to open uninhibited, and there was no real downside. A step down to enter the shed was inevitable — we simply moved it back a couple of feet (above photos).

With the basic question of where to place the shed out of the way, we went on to narrow down what the

Envisioning the exterior:

Salt Lake City is full of hundred-year-old homes that are embellished with what it often termed "Victorian Eclectic" elements. This can be broken down into a couple of major elements: fancy trim, and eye-catching paint schemes. We envisioned a studio space that took inspiration from the kinds of colorful trim details found throughout Brit's neighborhood. I had a concept in mind, and did a scale drawing to help move the process forward. To make the details come to life, I

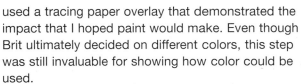

used a tracing paper overlay that demonstrated the impact that I hoped paint would make. Even though Brit ultimately decided on different colors, this step was still invaluable for showing how color could be used.

Early on, Brit showed me a pair of handmade stained glass windows that she had gotten from a friend and stored for a few years — we decided right away to integrate them into the shed's exterior. We considered placing them on different walls, but eventually decide that we could create an even bigger

visual impact by stacking them vertically. This turned into a lovely focal point on the front of the shed.

We also wanted at least two additional windows to both let in light and serve as elements that could be adorned with some colorful wood trim. It was important to Brit that the windows be small enough that they couldn't be security risks: to accomplish this, we adjusted the dimensions of one window to be too small and skinny to prevent entry from potential no-goodniks, and we placed the other window high up below the eaves. Using two trim colors meant that

we had to do a bit of masking as we painted, but the crisp result was worth the extra effort.

As a finishing touch to the exterior, Brit picked out a neat little lantern that we hung from a bracket that I made on-site (above). I think it adds a nice bit of charm.

Interior design elements:

The original plan called for painting the interior of the shed white in order to brighten up the interior, but it turned out that the windows and large doors let in plenty of light already, so this step was deemed unnecessary. The thick rug does double duty: visually, it adds a burst of color and warmth, and acoustically, it provides just enough sound-dampening to aid in the recording process. Brit and Jimmy also decided that they liked the look of the wood sheathing and studs. The colorful posters, in addition to commemorating various concerts and festivals from the past, provide a lot of character so that the interior of the shed has a vibrant character that matches the exterior. In fact, this

arrangement reflects the original design brief for the exterior finishes: lots of natural wood, with some fun accent colors applied in a restrained but bold way.

Since the shed was built as a DIY project to house a DIY recording project, it made sense to carry this ethos all the way through. Brit got crafty and made this mike stand from some odds and ends she had on hand (left). The band usually performs in settings where no amplification is required, but if it is, they cluster around a single mike, adjusting their individual volume levels by moving closer or farther from it. When they record, they do the same thing. This is more or less the old-time way, which originated in the days before technology allowed artists to record in-struments individually and then mix them together in a finished track. It is the simplest method, and Brit's band finds it to be just fine — they like the simplic-ity and earnestness of this approach, and are con-vinced that a more technologically sophisticated setup wouldn't really improve their end result.

The roof is supported by five site-made trusses that I made from 2x4's. They are basically rafters that are attached at the peak with plates I made from scrap plywwod (below). The cedar-shake roof (right) is practical, durable and beautiful. I finished it off with a galvanized cap to keep the ridge tightly sealed against the elements.

GALLERY

Photo Courtesy of Jase Man

Trying to find a shed that is traditional but not stodgy? Look no further. The translucent roofing lets in a ton of light, as well as adding a more modern touch to a classic design. The French doors and over-sized windows also help to create an interior that is bright and airy. The space at right feels much larger not only because of the abundant natural light, but because of the visual connection with the outdoors.

Photo Courtesy of Jase

The rough-hewn look of these sheds feels just right when it is combined with the bright colors used on the doors.

Photo Courtesy of John Smith

Tucked into the corner of the yard, this shed feels perfectly sited, also thanks in part to the mature plantings that surround it. Its scale also seems just right, given that it is surrounded by unusually tall fences (7' on the side and 8' behind it.)

This timber-framed shed is sided with locally-harvested rough pine boards. The transom windows (there is an identical one of the back side) brighten up the interior.

CHAPTER SIX

Guest House

My clients Shawn and Terri are really fun people, and because they're not originally from this area, they have a large network of friends from all over the country who are always eager to visit. This means that they have a lot of house guests, and they plan to keep on hosting people. In fact, Terri's mother-in-law has become a frequent visitor since the arrival of Luca, their two year old son. The only problem was the size of their house, which was around 1000sf. They have lived in their charming Victorian in downtown Salt Lake City for almost six years, and while they'd like to put on an addition, financing for a project like that is tough in today's economic climate. But they are optimistic folks, and if they couldn't afford to tackle a major project right now, they wondered if they might be able to still achieve some real lifestyle gains by executing a smaller scale one. Hence, the idea of the mini-guest house was born.

They envisioned a small outbuilding that could function as a sort of stop-gap measure to bridge the time span between now and the day that they hope to put on a significant addition, which will probably be seven-to-eight years from now. They understood this guesthouse wouldn't be able to have all of the features that the addition will — guests will still need to head in to the main house to use the bathroom or cook a meal — but on a small budget (under $1500), the couple hoped to at least improve their situation. The outbuilding could at least provide separate

sleeping and lounging areas for their guests, which will give everybody some much-needed privacy. And while they haven't tackled it yet, they've been tossing around the idea of an outdoor shower, which would be kind of novel.

This was the sorry state of the shed when I first saw it. Shawn had high hopes of finishing it on its own, but his schedule just wasn't going to allow it. He had taken to using it to store salvaged construction materials that he imagined himself using for the project.

Shawn is fairly handy, and he had begun work on the structure on his own, but his busy schedule and his new duties as a dad have kept him from giving it the attention he hoped for. That was when they contacted me, and I helped them jumpstart the foundering project and get it done — just in time for Grandma's two-week summer visit, fortunately.

When I arrived, the guesthouse was in tough shape — it had never really been properly buttoned up, and the only roof was some badly warped OSB sheathing. My first efforts were geared toward getting these big picture structural issues addressed, and then we set our sights on getting the interior finished off. Before we put up the drywall, I made sure to run some romex so that some basic electric service could be established. With Shawn available to help me drywall, this portion of the project went fairly quickly. Trying to drywall the ceiling by myself would've been a drag, although I suppose I could've rented a drywall lift for around $50. The rest of the interior was easy to finish, as there is very little in the way of trim or other embellishments.

As for heat, well, that is one of the drawbacks of the guesthouse in its current form. Shawn hopes to put in a small woodstove when the time is right — they have a spot picked out for it — and they figure that might make it an enticing place for winter guests. Terri isn't convinced, however, so for this reason, the structure is mostly useable for about half of the year. That can either be viewed as a glass half full or half empty situation, and they definitely agree that it is a step in the right direction.

They still hope to break ground on an addition to the main house, but since it won't be for a while, the guesthouse seems to have been a good idea in the meantime. In fact, Shawn and Terri have taken to using the shed for their own purposes. "It's a nice little get-away," says Terri, "And with such a small house, we're grateful for anything that gives us some more room to breathe."

(TOP) The shed was only partially sheathed when I arrived, so the first task was to properly dry in the exterior. (BOTTOM) There was quite a bit of daylight visible from inside — which is fine when it is coming from windows or doors, but in this case there was a fair bit of repair work to be done. Fortunately, I got involved before the shed had gone too far downhill to be salvaged.

The French doors were a great salvage find. They provide a very open feeling, which is appreciable in a small space like this.

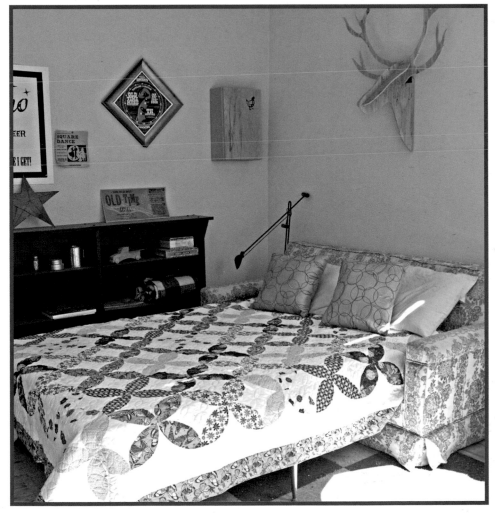

Terri and Shawn loved the slab coffee table, as did I, but it ultimately proved a bit impractical: it was just too heavy to move around when it came time to fold-out the bed! They have since substituted a smaller and lighter one in its place.

The bed pulled out. Sheets, blankets, and pillows are all stored in a cabinet in the guesthouse for the sake of user-friendliness.

The couch is a pullout, so it accommodates two adults for sleeping. Even with the bed extended, there is still plenty of room to move around. "Frankly," says Shawn, "I think it might just be a skootch bigger than our master bedroom inside. The plywood deer head is a tongue-in-cheek homage to the hunting trips Shawn used to take growing up in Northern Wisconsin."

Terri is an artist and interior designer, and she spent a bit of time mocking up a prototype for a light fixture. As they still haven't had the chance to finish running electricity out there, they took down the prototype, but I don't doubt that she'll get around to finishing that part of the project.

(OPPOSITE) Decorating the guesthouse was pretty easy — since Shawn and Terri have a pretty small house, it wasn't hard to find plenty of "overflow" décor items that could be moved along into the new space. The old sofa — which they like for its retro look — was a thrift store find, however.

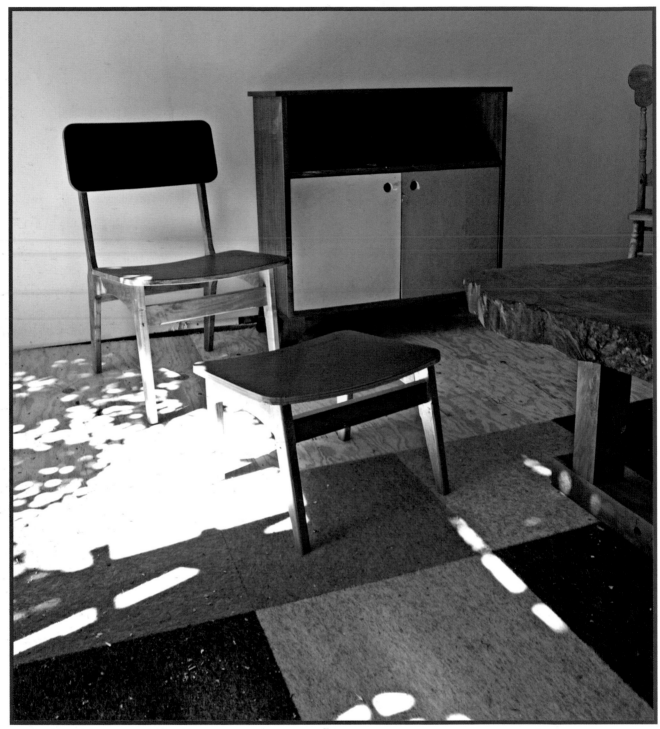

The carpeting is actually a mosaic made of modular tiles made by Flor. They are extremely durable, and are made by an environmentally conscious company, which Terri really likes. Another nice benefit is that individual tiles can be pulled out and replaced if they're ever heavily soiled or damaged beyond repair.

(OPPOSITE) As a symbol of their excitement about getting the shed finished, Shawn and Terri planted a cherry tree. It will be awhile before it bears any fruit, but they figure that it will look pretty neat as it grows up. This photo also shows the one-of-a-kind window that Shawn made. It makes for kind of a cool focal point. Raising backyard chickens has become pretty popular in Salt Lake City over the past few years, and the guesthouse shares space with the chickens that Shawn and Terri have raised since they were baby chicks. Keeping the doors shut is essential, however, because the chickens can mess up the interior in a hurry if they're allowed in.

GALLERY

Photo Courtesy of Charity Duncan

This unusual shed sits at the top of a knoll in the woods, and the approach is pretty dramatic, as the photo indicates. Where you put the shed often has as much of an impact as how you build it. The cow skull is an intriguing adornment.

I've never seen a roofline quite like this. In addition to being eye-catching, I imagine that the shape keeps the interior pretty open and useable.

Photo Courtesy of Steve & Jenna Copely

The concept of "annexing" the space adjacent to a shed by putting a roof over it is a great and often inexpensive way of increasing the shed's impact. You can create a separate area for entertaining, relaxing, storage, or working, depending on your needs.

This shed obviously wouldn't work too well as a year-round home office, for example, but as a stop along the way on a long bike ride? Looks like a perfect campsite to me.

Just because a tin roof is rusty doesn't mean it isn't water-tight: a lot of the time, the corrosion is limited to the surface of the metal and it is still perfectly useable. No roof lasts forever, but this one still has some life left in it, and metal (whether galvanized or factory-painted) are generally a pretty durable choice.

CHAPTER SEVEN
Gardener's Paradise

Kate Taylor is a serious gardener, and has been for a long time. Since moving into her home five years ago, she has transformed every nook and cranny into a home for plants of all kinds — especially fruits and vegetables. She has installed numerous raised beds, constructed a chicken coop and run, and set up a compost bin to enrich the soil — and this is just a partial list of her accomplishments in the yard. As she is both an enthusiastic cook and a fan of sustainable practices in whatever form they take, Kate loves being able to grow most of the produce that her family consumes. And since a gardener's work is never done, and she still has plans for all kinds of new crops and different ways to grow them, she began to think about how nice it would be to have a great shed that could double as a workroom and greenhouse. Much more than a place just to store a couple of shovels, Kate began to scheme about a gardener's paradise. Over time, she began to list her ideas, and she eventually asked me to be part of the process. Our first planning session paved the way for a very successful project.

The first thing we did was to take stock of the potential sites. The most promising was along a fence line at the side of the yard. This happened to be the home of a pre-fab plastic shed that Kate was eager to replace, and it also had a nice southern exposure which looked ideal for a greenhouse. In light of this (pun intended), we decided to place the shed toward the back of the yard, with the greenhouse attached to its south side. Our design called for a greenhouse roof that sloped in one flat plane, and so the tallest wall would be the wall that it shared with the shed; for this reason, we decided that that was a logical place to put the door. We also wanted to run floor-to-ceiling shelves along the glass walls, so that further eliminated those walls of the greenhouse as possible places to put a door. The decision to use this kind of layout was cemented by the realization that the shed and greenhouse are functionally linked — there was bound to be some carrying back-and-forth of equipment and whatnot from one to the other. The two are separated by an operable door so that the greenhouse can be closed off without letting too much heat into the shed during the cold winter months.

With the overall layout shaping up, we began to talk about some of the specific features that Kate hoped to incorporate. Kate had lots of other suggestions involving the shed's functionality: she hoped for a large potting bench with plenty of elbow room, and a large open storage space below the benchtop to store straw for her chickens, Finding a good place for this had been a challenge, so integrating it here would be a big help, We were able to devote a lot of space to the bench by wrapping it along the walls in a "L" shaped configuration (opposite).

One of the most unusual was a sink that she could use for a number of different things. She envisioned it as very useful for a variety of food-growing and prep tasks. It would be an easy way to supply water for the greenhouse, for one thing, and it would also come in handy at mealtime. It has worked out as she had hoped: vegetables can be picked directly from the garden, rinsed in the sink, and taken directly to the table or grill. This is a convenient time-saver, and it also makes it easy for other people to participate in preparing dinner. Guests can make a salad without setting foot in the kitchen, where, I am told, too many cooks can spoil the soup.

In addition, Kate figured that having a sink out there would allow her to use the shed as a workspace for homebrewing and wine-making from her own grapes. She ended up finding a really cool old sink and faucet

at an architectural salvage business in town for under $20. Not only is this a fraction of what it would've cost new, but she got the satisfaction of being able to reuse some perfectly good old fixtures. In the spirit of keeping things simple, Kate suggested that the sink just drain into a removable bucket, which could then be moved around the yard to water plants or animals as need be. A consideration like this may not sound like much in some of the wetter parts of the country, but in a low-rainfall area like Utah, it is a really practical idea.

I also built a tall cabinet to store home-brewing supplies, and I placed it in the corner where it would be most out of the way. A chalkboard on the front of the cabinet provided a handy place to write notes and reminders (below).

In addition to discussing the practical features that the shed would need, we spent a lot of time discussing its overall design and aesthetic. We talked about different rooflines and how they influence the look and feel of the building. Ultimately, Kate decided that a shed roof, sloped toward the back of the property, would provide the most head height and also allow for a row of transom windows above the double doors. The transom windows serve to bring in quite a lot of light, and they also add character to the exterior above).

We also planned for an overhanging roof on the front of the shed to create a "front porch" area as a transition to the rest of the yard. We ultimately decided to construct this as a trellis so that it could provide a good home for some grapevines, from which Kate plans to make wine in a few years once the vines have been established and are producing well (right).

We also wanted the interior to be versatile, with plenty of easily accessible storage in general for stuff

THE GREENHOUSE

Structurally, the greenhouse is made of 2x4 walls that provide a place to anchor the recycled windows. The roof is put together in the same way. Some of the windows are operable — it will be helpful to be able to control heat and humidity at certain times of the year — but most of them are fixed, which makes the walls quite rigid. Kate found the windows on Craigslist, and negotiated to buy them all for under $100. I thought it was a great score. Not only was the quantity sufficient to build the entire greenhouse, with a few leftover to construct a nice-sized coldframe, but the windows have a quaint, old-fashioned character that looks cool.

To maximize the amount of shelving, I built two large units that run along the glass sides of the greenhouse. The greenhouse is small, and more shelving could be added later, but we decided to start with this, due to the fact that some open floor space is kind of nice to have just so you're not too cramped while working in there.

The shed is equipped with a gutter along the back edge, which will help to manage water in the area. The gutter drains to a bucket inside the greenhouse to minimize the work of hauling water around during the winter. If the volume of water should ever be too much, the flexible downspout will allow the water to be directed elsewhere.

of all sizes. We knew that Kate would need to accommodate both large garden tools and also lots of small stuff like seed containers. Pegboard provided an inexpensive way to set up flexible storage and display, and it can easily be reconfigured as need be, so we went with it (left).

The overall plan called for a shed that was funky and a little bit rough. Something overly fussy or prim just wasn't the goal. To achieve this, we identified a materials palette of rough cedar board and batten siding, brightly painted trim, and galvanized steel roofing. To add a burst of color to the interior, I painted a lot of the woodwork red. This also seemed like a neat reference to traditional agrarian buildings. Come to think of it, this is probably why the color was called "barn red".

Incorporating the star cutout in a boldly painted blue panel was a touch of whimsy that emerged rather serendipitously: I needed to install the panel to fill the space above the window, and it suddenly occurred to me that it would be a neat spot for an iconic shape. The cutout serves to let in light, as a small bonus.

We liked the idea of dutch doors on the front of the shed, and we accomplished this by hinging the top halves of the doors independently from the bottoms. To allow the doors to function normally, these simple latches hold the top and bottom halves together.

Double doors maximize the amount of light and fresh air, sense of spaciousness and connection to the surrounding yard. This would also be handy in case any really large items needed to be moved into or out of the shed. On a daily basis, however, only one door is used, and the other is held closed by a large L-shaped piece of hardware that secures into the floor.

This old pitchfork actually gets used from time to time, but when it isn't pressed into service turning over compost, it serves as an ideal design accessory on the front of the building.

The area below the shed's roof is left open to allow some air circulation on hot summer days. If it turns out to be a problem for some unforeseen reason, it would be easy to block it up.

The transom windows look great, and they also provided a neat place to attach some trim that we could paint in a bold color. We tried to balance the amount of wood siding with the painted trim.

(OPPOSITE) By ending the workbench short of the far wall, we created a floor-to-ceiling nook that would be perfect for storing tall, thin tools like rakes.

To keep seeds in one place, I built this simple box from reclaimed tin ceiling tiles and affixed it to the wall. It has a look that fits in neatly with the other interior finsishes.

The pegboard walls provided more than just storage: they also made it easy to hang herbs for drying and small decorative knick-knacks.

To save money, I made the cedar siding from 6' tall fence pickets. This was much less expensive than buying 8' long boards. To disguise the fact that the 6' pickets weren't long enough, I just added a short piece above them and covered the gap with a horizontal batten. The result is that it looks like it was planned that way from the beginning, and we saved about $70.

Running water to the shed was fairly simple. We used ½" Pex tubing, as it resists damage from freezing and is easy to work with.

To maximize storage space, we set this small bookshelf on the back of the workbench.

We tried to make everything look nice — even the interior door separating the shed from the greenhouse was dressed up with some reclaimed barn siding.

GALLERY

Photo Courtesy of Paul Downey

Quaint details like these one-of-a-kind glass doors provide a window both into and out of the shed. Initially built as a convalescence hut, I imagine that the original bed-ridden inhabitants preferred the view over that of a sterile hospital ward.

I'm not sure which is more interesting here, the fun colors or the repetition of the same simple form in this long line of beach-front sheds.

Photo Courtesy of Les Chatfield

Who says a shed needs to be given a whole corner of a yard? The shed was custom-built to slip into a pre-existing void below the house, and it created a much better way to use the space.

Photo Courtesy of Dennis & Aimee Jonez

Photo Courtesy of Erich Ferdinand

Photo Courtesy of Peyri Herrera

Although the building itself is almost stark because of its very minimal level of detailing applied to its exterior, the site still comes across as very approachable because of all the greenery and the patio in front. It is a neat juxtaposition of rigid and organic elements.

The deep roof overhang and protruding beams would make this building a fine accompaniment to an Arts & Crafts style home, which shares similar design elements.

The Bike Guy is the opposite of a glitzy corporate chain store. Their down-to-earth workspace and attitudes are a couple of things that their clients really like about them. Built four years ago, Johnny did the site prep and concrete work. A client, who is a contractor, put up the structure in about two days. Johnny and his wife have done all of the work to finish out the interior, including the drywall.

CHAPTER EIGHT

The Bike Guy

Located in a shed next to their home in the vibrant and eclectic Sugarhouse neighborhood of Salt Lake City, Johnny Barlow and his wife Elva Nava run a successful small business that shows what is possible when you get creative, work hard — and put up a great shed. A veteran bike mechanic, Johnny began doing tune-ups in their yard, and the couple eventually decided that having a proper building would provide the boost necessary to make the business viable year-round. The solution that they've engineered keeps their overhead manageable and helps them to enjoy a lifestyle of their own design.

Johnny's racing days are in the past, but this photo proves they were real: here he was at the 1997 NORBA Nationals in Deer Valley, Utah.

A prestigious local award from Salt Lake magazine in 2008 was a huge coup in terms of exposure.

Johnny has been active in the world of bicycles for a long time, and he's deeply familiar with it from a variety of perspectives. He got into mountain biking in the late 80's, and this led him into racing. In 1991, he attended the United Bicycle Institute, where he spent two weeks learning the skills that he has spent the last twenty years refining. During his racing years he worked in shops — the employee discount made it possible for him to afford the best. However, spending a lot of time around high-performance bicycles turned him into a bit of a bike snob, he now admits with a laugh. He spent a number of years looking down his nose at anything but the most high-end bikes and accessories, but his attitude has evolved a great deal since then.

As he moved on in life, Johnny began to think more about the vast segment of society whose bike needs aren't in the spotlight cast by elite athletes, and he came to recognize the value of bikes as more than just another status symbol: a bike doesn't have to be expensive to provide fun, exercise and transportation. And while Johnny still does his share of work on high-end bikes, he spends a lot of time working on bikes for regular folks, too. This has led him toward a role in advocacy within the bicycle community. Salt Lake City, like many other places in the country, has a lot of residents who appreciate bike paths, bike lanes and a culture that supports safe cycling, and Johnny often attends meetings of the Mayor's Bicycle Advisory Council and the Salt Lake County Bicycle Advisory Committee. I've noticed that Johnny spends a lot of time talking to his customers and getting to know them — I think that this person-to-person contact might be one of his most valuable legacies in the

By storing wheels, tires, and more overhead, Johnny and Elva are able to make the most of their tight space.

Even though it takes up a bit more space, Johnny likes to hang up some of his fancier tools. Their mechanisms are quite sensitive and could easily be damaged in a cluttered drawer.

Business Shed

Johnny's business is very visible, which helps bring in new clients, but it also means that he has learned to work within local business and zoning regulations — he encourages anybody who is thinking about starting a shed-based business to do the same. At first glance, this may seem like an obstacle for a new business owner, but Johnny has seen that this isn't the case at all: he's gotten a lot of support from encouraging city officials who really want him to succeed.

The large skylight lets in a ton of natural light. Without it, it would be tough to keep things organized in the rear of the shed. Looking up at the skylight seemed to put Johnny in a wistful mood. For as much progress as they've made, he reflected, they're never really done, either. They plan to insulate the roof soon, which should make a big difference in keeping the temperatures comfortable inside.

The tightly-packed feel of the shop is part of its charm.

community. Passionate conversations between people interested in making positive change happen have always been the lifeblood of grassroots activism.

Over the past few years, Johnny has been joined by his wife Elva Nava, who now works side-by-side with him. She picked up a lot from watching him and assisting over the years, and having paid her dues, she has become a great mechanic in her own right. They joke around that the name "Bike Guy" doesn't really fit anymore, but its hardly a major problem. Their reputation will keep clients coming in regardless of the business name. In addition to nurturing their young business, the couple has two young children, with whom they're able to spend a lot of time, thanks to their really short commute. I can only imagine how fun it must be to grow up in a colorful setting like this, surrounded by bikes and the interesting people who bring them in for a tune-up from the Bike Guy.

Johnny and Elva are obsessive about keeping their tools organized and maintained. This wasn't a staged photo — they're always this carefully arranged.

This station (above) is dedicated to wheel-building and truing. Its location in the shop is partly determined by the quality of light that it receives from the skylight, as the precise nature of the work done there depends on it.

Johnny and Elva offer a nice array of components and accessories in the retail area (left). This winter, they will be adding on more slatwall to provide more retail display, which should help to boost sales and allow them to carry a larger inventory. I hadn't noticed until they pointed it out, but the slatwall in this photo is handmade, thanks to Johnny's circular saw and crafty mind.

During the summer months, they're so busy that they encourage clients to make appointments — they actually have to turn away business because the demand is so high. In the wintertime, Johnny and Elva offer ski and snowboard tuning services, which is pretty sought after in our community where skiing is a way of life for a lot of people for six months out of the year. This high-tech tuning machine makes it possible — in the winter time, they pull it out and it takes center stage.

They usually tune skis in batches: there is a lot of prep work in getting the equipment running perfectly, so it makes sense to do a whole bunch at a time.

Snowboards require a separate workstation; during the winter time, this is a critical part of their business.

GALLERY

The uses you might find for a small outbuilding are limited only by your imagination. In parts of rural Russia, tiny chapels such as this are not uncommon.

Photo Courtesy of Ezio Man

Building a shed with a loft isn't hard — if you plan for it from the beginning, you can easily add on a bonus space up in the eaves.

Photo Courtesy of Seamus Holman

This calm, composed space is enhanced by the restrained combination of painted trim and natural siding. The circular pattern in the brick floor is echoed in the circular window and the drop-leaf table.

Jay Shafer has spent nearly fifteen years building and promoting what has come to be known as the "small house lifestyle". His tiny dwellings are works of art, with an incredible level of attention to detail.

The long overhangs on this rustic retreat also perform a practical function: they help the roof to shed snow away from the building, which prevents premature wear on the siding. Wooden elements of the structure that are over-exposed to moisture will be more prone to rot and require more frequent repainting or staining.

CHAPTER NINE

Violin Maker's Shop

Salt Lake City is home to the Violin Maker's School of America, one of only a handful of such institutions in the world, and as a result, we have a much higher than normal per capita number of violin makers. People come from all over the world to study the craft, and lots of them end up sticking around. To help keep their expenses down, a pair of recent graduates — Kristian and Bryan — have joined forces and set up a shop in a shed in Bryan's backyard. The workspaces are small, and they hope that they'll be able to upgrade to larger quarters in the future, but this solution seems to be working out well enough that they have each constructed a number of violins in the 10 months that they had occupied the shop. The shed is divided into two tiny rooms, and each artisan has his own, although the division isn't hard and fast; they're always working together, bouncing ideas off of each other, and providing feedback during their workdays. Overall, their arrangement seems to be working out fine, and they both find it preferable to the higher expenses that larger spaces would require.

Because he's really tall, Bryan's bench is, too. When you spend all day standing in one spot doing challenging work, having the ergonomics dialed in is essential.

Kristian has the smaller room, and the space is adequate, but the major disadvantage is the lack of natural light. To compensate, Kristian has set up a bunch of lights that he can turn on and off to suit his needs at a given time. To make up for this drawback, Bryan gives him a break on the rent, which, Kristian acknowledges, comes in handy. They both told me a story about a very well-known violin maker who is famous for working in a really dark studio, because he spent his first couple of years making instruments in a basement with only one overhead light and no windows. They take this anecdote as a source of inspiration, or at the very least, humor.

Kristian's bench is adequate, but he had to bolt it to the floor when he moved it. Beforehand, it just wasn't sturdy enough.

These guys take sharpening to a whole new level. Because they rely almost entirely on hand tools, it is critical that the tools are really well maintained. I used one of Kristian's chisels once and immediately realized how bad I am at sharpening — if they saw my chisels, I'd probably die of embarassment. Having one really well-appointed sharpening station rather than two saves both space and money; the pair actually purchased the Tormek sharpener together, and when they eventually part ways, they'll fight over custody then

Fortunately, Kristian isn't a real pack rat, because there isn't a lot of storage space. These second-hand shelves work out fine for storing the templates, jigs, and other assorted supplies that he uses on a regular basis.

Although they share some equipment — a bandsaw, sharpener, bending irons, for example — each luthier owns and maintains his own set of hand tools, including planes, scrapers, and all manner of chisels.

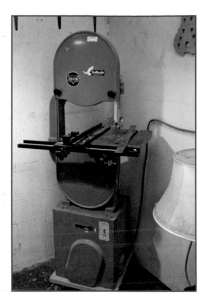

If they were building furniture or cabinetry, they'd most likely need a lot more space to be able to accommodate the large tools that those pursuits require, but because they're mostly hand tool guys, they can squeeze into a smaller space and make it work. Their only large power tool is the bandsaw that Bryan purchased from a local university surplus program

The work is carried out by the same methods that have been in use for hundreds of years. The spruce top (near) and maple back (far) are fine-tuned using tiny finger planes that are barely an inch long.

One of Kristian's first moves was installing the shelf high up on the wall. When you don't have a lot of storage space, every little bit helps. I think he may have gone overboard with the brackets, though, unless that stereo is a lot heavier than it looks.

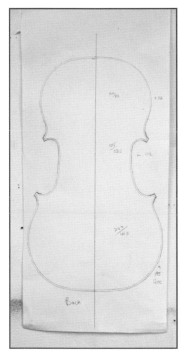

Every instrument that they build starts out as a full-sized drawing, which then needs to be on display until the work is complete.

These violins are nearly finished. When they're done, they can be setup and shipped to high-end instrument dealers around the country on their way to a permanent home. Because of this arrangement, Bryan and Kristian don't need any kind of showroom of their own, and this helps keep their overhead affordable.

Since Bryan's room is slightly larger, it is home to a desk where the pair can conduct business. It isn't fancy, but it is all they need.

The hand tools in Bryan's room resembles Kristian's to the untrained eye, but I'm sure they could point out all kinds of nuances.

For joining the large pieces of wood that they glue up to make the front and back plates of the each violin, they secure a plane upside-down in a vise. This approach allows them to quickly achieve the results they need in a low-tech and space-efficient way.

Nope, it isn't firewood. These rough slabs will be transformed into the front and back of a full-size standup bass.

GALLERY

Yes, the lower left photo was shown earlier, but seeing it from the side (above) offers a different perspective. By constructing a house directly atop a trailer, it is easily movable. It also may mean that things like building permits are irrelevant (check with the building department in your area to be sure).

The exterior finishes on this tiny house are quite durable and practical. The roof is even set up for rainwater collection, which would be a great way to help water a garden, among other things.

Photos Courtesy of Nicolas Boullosa

If you like a cozy interior, this one's for you. Looks like a terrific place to relax with a book.

Every inch of the tiny house interiors are carefully thought out and constructed. This corner bookshelf is ideal for both storage and display.

CHAPTER TEN

Fancy Built

Even though I had seen photos of their work online, I was still astonished at the level of creativity — hand-in-hand with top-notch workmanship — when I saw one of their playhouses in person.

Their story below (excerpted from fancybuilt.com) is a fascinating one, and it is a perfect example of how a humble outbuilding can be designed and built into a thing of beauty.

I was fortunate to be able to witness the installation of one of their signature playhouses. It had been fabricated in their shop, and arrived in two pieces. (A small amount of finish work is done on-site, but most of the construction occurs beforehand).

From Custom Homes to Custom Outbuildings

Sergei, the "Fancy Builder" himself, had been building custom homes for 16 years when the housing market crashed in 2008 and suddenly they found they needed to do something else to provide for their family. They soon found the perfect outlet for all their creative skills they had developed when building fancy houses. "Fancy Built — Playful Outbuildings" started out as a family side business with Sergei and his dad, Nikolay,

building sheds and playhouses for local customers. They found that every person has different ideas about what they want in their shed or playhouse or chicken coop. Their niche is in building exactly what the customer wants while working within their family's budget. They stick with the project from the early dream/design stage in the beginning to the final building and set-up at the end.

Jen is the designer. She works one-on-

A concrete pad had been poured beforehand and was ready for the installation.

Sergei usually uses a crane to lift the upper section into place — the cable on top of the roof provides a sturdy place to hook it up. On this particular job site, another contractor had a small excavator that they used to do the heavy lifting.

one with the customer, keeping in constant contact via phone and e-mail to design the perfect outbuilding that fits their unique needs. She can draw up a shed that matches a house or a playhouse that matches a drawing in the customer's daughter's favorite storybook.

Sergei is the master builder and with the help of the crew they can build anything you can imagine. Literally! Not only does Sergei have experience building custom million dollar homes but he has also worked on several movie sets, commercial projects and the 2002 Salt Lake City Olympics. Most recently he has built the alien city for the new Disney movie, "John Carter of Mars" near Lake Powell, UT as well as a permanent outdoor movie set of the city of Jerusalem (covering almost seven acres) for the Church of Latter Day Saints.

Jen and Sergei have five kids so they know what kids want (and what they can do to play structures!) They also have a milk cow, a dog and a flock of friendly chickens on their 2-1/2 acre "hobby farm." Their dream is to spend more time together at home, raising their kids, raising a garden and beautifying their little piece of heaven on earth.

Designing and building playful outbuildings is what they do for fun and fitness (and to finance their dream). They have really enjoyed meeting and getting to know each one of their customers from the owner of the farmer's market in Pocatello, Idaho, to the family with nine children in Alpine, UT.

The "Bavarian Cottage Playhouse" shown here, was featured on the NBC game show, "It's Worth What?" in September 2011.

The interior of the playhouse absolutely blew me away. The upstairs even has a secret room cleverly concealed behind a painting that swings out of the way to reveal a door (right).

The table and chairs (above)provide space for all kinds of projects. The ground floor of the playhouse (right) is roomy enough to accommodate a really cute play kitchen set.

The curved rooflines lend the perfect touch of whimsy to the overall design. These two were clearly in love with the place!

The exterior corners of the first floor are dressed up with cultured stone. The attention to detail was comparable to what I've seen on fine homes in the area!

This Bavarian cottage is covered with thoughtful details: the hand-carving on this window, as well as the bold red paint on the frame, are really eye-catching.

I wish my own house had a lamp this nice next to the front door! The playhouses are all wired for electricity, and the lights actually work.

Not only does the playhouse feature a balcony on the second story, but an ingenious hoist has been installed that allows kids to haul a bucket up from the ground floor.

If all you saw was this photo, you could easily be fooled into thinking that you're looking at a full-size home in a high-end neighborhood.

WINDOWS & DOORS

This shed fits quietly into the landscape, but the way the tall curved doors fit into their openings is somehow elegant, nonetheless.

The warbly, handmade quality of this glass compliments the rustic character of the shed perfectly. It is a tiny detail that makes you want to get up close to check out.

This door is reminiscent of old-fashioned doors on a turn-of-the-century carriage house.

This elaborate trim is a great embellishment for a kids' play-house. It is also simpler than it looks at first glance: the window trim isn't actually made from separate pieces of wood, as one might assume; it is created by routing an outline and then painting the "trim" brown.

This fanciful window looks great and works well. At the heart of the unit is a vinyl-clad, double-paned window, and the elaborate trim gives it a whimsical feel.

These transom window openings below the eaves let a lot of light into the shed without compromising security at all.

Speaking of eclectic … the way that this window and door are positioned so close together made for a quirky arrangement of the trim elements.

Because it uses a standard locking handset, it is easy to secure this shed without resorting to a padlock and hasp.

This handmade vent still functions perfectly in allowing the users to regulate airflow.

Talk about a surprising constrast: the bright, colorful patterns on this door are an amazing way to lend some drama to this otherwise rough and understated exterior.

A classic dutch door. The oversized strap hinges and the variation in the woodworking (compare the "X" braces on the top and bottom) provide an artisanal, handmade feel.

The quintessential barn window: this iconic detail says a lot about the rest of the structure.

This window draws you in and makes you wonder about the building's history: the glass window is a replacement set behind the original window frame. How come? And by whom?

It isn't all about the view from outside: a well-placed window can frame a view that makes spending time in a small outbuilding all the more enchanting.

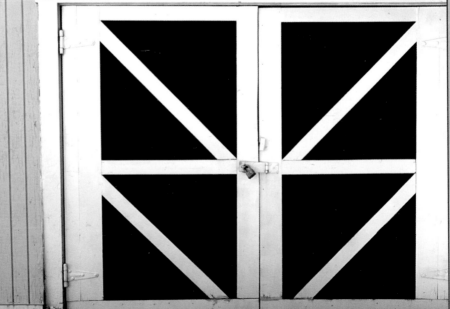

When it comes to maintenance, do you keep the paint looking fresh with occasional recoating, or let it age gracefully? The bold color on these doors makes a powerful statement.

This elaborate trim was probably amazing back when it was in better shape. The simplicity of the window — basic slab construction, with no trim or adornment — helps to keep the focus on the diamond pattern.

Neither overly traditional or modern, this window treatment is pretty versatile. The casing is made from the same cedar used for siding, and the dark trim on the window itself is quite understated.

The zippy, purple, trim paint makes it an eye-catcher, as is the zinc plated hardware.

ROOFING

Most of the time, a shed's roof is pretty visible, and thus the material that you choose will make a real difference aesthetically. While there is a wide range of pricing, depending on the material, most shed roofs are pretty small, so the quantity required might be small enough to justify spending a bit more if you really have your heart set on something spendy. Here's a brief summary of some of the options you might wish to consider:

Cedar Shakes

Cedar is one of the best natural roofing materials available, sometimes lasting over 70 years. The natural oils found in cedar help reduce the risk of wood rot and insect damage, while its straight grain helps to ensure that the shakes will remain flat and stable. Also, you don't need to seal the shakes — left untreated, they will weather to a rich and rustic gray. If you do wish to preserve the original look of the shakes, you can apply a sealer every year or so.

Asphalt Shingles

This is by far the more ubiquitous roofing material in America, which is mostly because it is affordable and performs very well. Available in a range of colors and textures, asphalt shingles should last for decades with no maintenance.

Galvanized Corrugated Tin

Traditionally used on agricultural buildings, and more recently prized by the modern design crowd, these panels are usually two-to-three feet wide, and they can be found in lengths from 8-14'. This means that you can quickly cover a lot of ground with this type of roofing, and the cost is quite reasonable as well. You'll want to make sure to use screws with rubber grommets to secure it to the sheathing. You can increase the amount of light in the building by substituting clear corrugated pvc panels for some of the galvanized ones.

patti pitzer

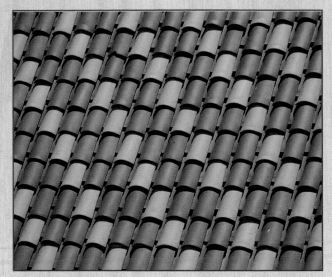

Clay Tile Roofing

A standard Spanish Colonial treatment, this type of roofing is very labor-intensive to install, and it is consequently not a budget-conscious choice. That said, a small outbuilding might not require a large amount, so the overall price might still work. If you're interested, it can't hurt to get some estimates.

Standing Seam Roofing

This premium roofing system is seen in mountainous areas because it sheds snow quite well. It is also extremely durable, and 40 year warranties are not uncommon. It is generally quite expensive.

Clear Plastic Roofing

This view of this unsheathed shed illustrates just how much light the clear PVC roofing lets it.

Green Roofs

Also known as living roofs, these wild and wooly designs are becoming more and more popular. The type that is best suited to a small building like a shed is categorized as an Extensive roof, as it is designed to be virtually self-sustaining and require low to no-maintenance. It needs a planting medium of one-to-four inches on a flat or gently sloping roof. It works best with native vegetation or drought-resistant, cold-resistent, shallow-rooted plants, sedum, herbs, mosses or grass which generally grow no higher than several inches. Such roofs typically weigh 10-50 lbs. per square foot, fully saturated, depending on what type of growing medium is used.

Roof Overhangs

I've seen a ton of pre-fab sheds that have almost no roof overhangs; to me, this is not only unattractive, but it is impractical. A roof overhang should extend enough so that water and snow that fall from the roof can drain away at a slight remove from the building. In some cases, large roof overhangs can help provide protection from oppressive sunlight during the hot summer months — this is a common technique in passive solar design. If you'd like to add some personality to the trim details of a shed, dressing up the rafter ends can look great, too. Embellished rafters are a major element of Arts & Crafts exteriors.

MONEY SAVERS

There are two big ways to save money: do the work (or a portion of it) yourself, and be resourceful with the furnishings and materials. If the existing building is fundamentally sound, and doesn't require too much in terms of structural modifications, you can probably plan to put most of your money into the aesthetic part of the project (aka the Fun Stuff). If you're starting from scratch, obviously a larger share of the budget will go into construction. Each project in this book will provide detail on how much money was spent, and what it went for — hopefully this will help you to see what is actually possible in the real world. I'll also provide some worksheets that might be useful in your own planning process. Even if you choose not to fill them out, I think you'll find that they may help you to ask the right questions and organize your thoughts. Note that not all of the categories may apply (for example, your shed may not need rain gutters) but I tried to be comprehensive so that the worksheet could apply to a diverse range of projects.

Build your own doors and windows

The amount you can spend on doors will vary considerably depending on how you go about it. If you're looking to save some money, I suggest you consider building your own doors. There is a large range of what is possible here — a quick and dirty door can be assembled with plywood and 2x4's in a half an hour for a cost of $25, or you could spend a bit more time and craft something with a lot of character if you're so inclined. Just bear in mind that paying someone else to build high-end doors will probably have a high price tag.

If you're interested in building simple non-operating windows, you can do this yourself on the cheap, too. Here's a straight-forward step-by-step process that you might want to try.

You'll first need to know the exterior dimensions of the window so that it will fit into its opening. I suggest making it ¼" smaller so that any discrepancies (i.e. an out-of-square opening) don't prevent your window from fitting. Once you have these dimensions, it is time to think backwards and calculate the size of the parts that you'll need to cut out. It is also good to know the relevant terminology: the sides of the window (running vertically) are referred to as the stiles, while the horizontal members are called rails. The length of the stiles is the same as the overall height of the window, while the length of the rails is equal to the width of the window minus (2 x the width of the stiles). With these dimensions worked out, you can mill the stiles and rails to size. This photo shows the relative positions of the stiles and rails.

When I build windows like this, I like to simply fit the glass into a groove that runs along the interior faces of the stiles and rails. This is much easier and quicker than applying glazing to the pane, and it creates a neat and clean look. I cut the groove with on my tablesaw. Depending on the width of your sawblade, you may need to make a couple of cuts side-by-side to make the glass fit.

RESOURCES

A-Shed USA

Denver, CO & Salt Lake City, UT

877-746-7274

www.a-shed.com

Backyard Buildings & More

Raleigh, NC

877-743-3400

www.backyardbuildings.com

Fancy Built - Playful Outbuildings

Payson, UT

801-592-1153

www.fancybuilt.com

The Home Depot

Atlanta, GA

800-466-3337

www.homedepot.com

Homestead Structures

New Holland, PA

877-272-7252

www.homesteadstructures.com

Lowes

North Wilkesboro, NC

800-445-6937

www.lowes.com

Outside Up/Mike Olfert

Portland OR

503-481-4484

www.outsideup.com

Sheds USA

Portsmouth, NH

866-616-2685

www.shedsusa.com

Tuff Shed

Denver, CO

866-860-8833

www.tuffshed.com

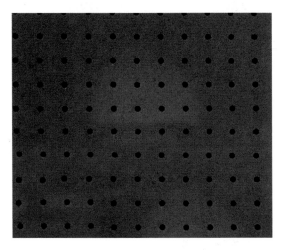

Helpful Outdoor Information

Designing For the Great Outdoors

If you're used to building furniture for the great indoors, you'll need to do a few things differently when it comes to projects that can withstand the wear and tear that the elements will impose. One of the most notable areas to pay attention to is in fastener selection — ordinary zinc-coated screws and bolts simply won't hold up outside. They'll rust and eventually fail. For this reason, I recommend fasteners made from stainless steel, or ones that are at least coated suitably to stand up to moisture. You may also want to choose materials that have a well-known track record for holding up agains the elements. While all of the species on the list below might not be available in your area, most people should have access to at least a few:

Decay-Resistant Species

Cedar
Cherrry (black)
Chestnut
Cypress (Arizona)
Ipe
Juniper
Locust (black)
Mahogany
Mesquite
Mulberry (red)
Oak (bur, chestnut Gambel, Oregon white, post and white)
Osage-orange
Redwood
Sassafras
Walnut (black)
Yew (Pacific)

Another area that merits some special attenion is the wide world of adhesives. For outdoor projects, I've used the following with good results:

- Polyurethane-type adhesives (Gorilla Glue)
- Titebond II and Titebond III
- Epoxy
- Construction adhesive

Every adhesive has its pros and cons. Here's a short list of tips that may help out:

Polyurethane glue will tend to produce a lot of foamy squeeze-out. This residue will have to be removed and I suggest using a wet sponge while the product is still wet. It also scrapes off easily with a chisel once it's dry.

When using polyurethane glue, if you get any glue on your hands, make sure to wash them throroughly while the glue is still wet — otherwise it'll have to wear off, and this can take a long time!

Construction adhesives can be a poor choice for precisely-fit joinery, but a very good solution for applications where gap-filling strength is advantageous.

The performance of all adhesives can be improved by increasing the amount of gluing surface. One way to do this is to use lapped joints.

Outdoor Wood Finishing

Protecting wood from the ravages of the elements is a tall order. It certainly can be done, and I'll recommend a couple of specific products that have a good track record, but first let me present what might be best called an inconvenient truth:

Every outdoor finish should be viewed as a temporary solution.

While I would love to be able to point toward a particular product or process that provides perfect results and lasts forever, such a magic solution just doesn't exist. So, be forewarned: finishes that are exposed to the elements will have to be periodically maintained, and if they aren't, the finishes will eventually fail and lookpretty crummy.

The main culprits are the twin demons of Ultraviolet spectrum light (UV) and moisture, and it often appears that the former creates just as much havoc as the latter. It's perhaps natural to assume that water poses a greater threat, but the opposite is often true: long exposure to sunlight — particularly at high altitudes — can be a finish's worst enemy. I know professional finishers who will turn down a project based on the amount of sunlight that the project will be exposed to, as they realize they're going to be called back after a short time to begin fighting an uphill battle.

So, the starting point in the quest to properly finish wood for the great outdoors has to begin by examining your expectations. Are you prepared to maintain (meaning scuff-sand and recoat) the finish every few years? Even the best finish will need attention every two-to-five years. Do you expect a refined finish that is similar to indoor furniture? If so, you'll need to apply a lot of coats to begin with, and you'll pay accordingly for a high-end finishing product. Or are you thinking about a more rustic project that will be allowed to age gracefully? These questions will help guide you to the right solution for your needs.

Specific Finishes

If you have some background with wood finishes, you're aware that most products come in one of two categories: penetrating oils; or film finishes. The names are apt descriptors. Penetrating oils, often tinted with stain, sink into the pores of the wood and are an effective way of changing wood's natural color. They are tempting because they're so easy to apply — just flood the surface and then wipe away the excess. Unfortunately, this ease of application comes at a price: they offer almost nothing in terms of protection against nature. Yes, they look good on day one, but over the course of even a single year, they offer basically no advantages to just doing nothing. Wood will tend to weather just as much as if it had been completely untreated.

Film finishes include varnishes, polyurethanes and lacquers. To hold up outdoors, many people turn to spar varnishes, with mixed results. They generally require at least four coats, and will probably need to be maintained yearly, depending on the weather in your area. I've had some poor results with spar varnish on some projects in my own backyard, but I probably needed a thicker build-up of the product — I did three coats on a small tabletop, and it had flaked off completely in less than a year. Or perhaps the surface wasn't clean enough to begin with, so the new finish never properly adhered to the wood. Epifanes was recently rated the best in comparison by a major woodworking magazine. Although the product was originally designed for use on wooden boats, it will hold up just fine on furniture and other outdoor woodwork. Beware, however, that simply choosing the best-rated product doesn't mean that the process will be easy: the manufacturer recommends six coats, which will take a while, since you'll need to allow a day between coats. Another approach that I've heard great things about is the Cetol system from Sikkens. It's a two-part system in that it recommends you use Cetol 1 as a base coat, and then two coats of Cetol 23 as a top coat. Three coats sound better than the six suggested for the Epifanes, and the cost is comparable between the two products.

If you don't mind stepping away from wood tones, paint is always a good option, and oil-based paints will hold up much better than later ones. I recommend using a semi-gloss finish so that the final surface will be easy to clean, and you'll want to take the time to apply a coat of exterior-rated primer first. I also suggest that the paint you choose is rated highly for color retention — not all exterior paints are created equal in this regard, and I've seen some that faded quite noticeably in just a couple of years.

What about deck stains? Nope. I've actually tried this approach with a set of dining chairs that I made for my own home four years ago. The stain colored the wood in a pleasing way, which was certainly one of my objectives, but the resulting finish was rough and not quite appropriate for furniture. It held up fine for a couple of years, and then it clearly needed another coat, because it had faded quite a bit and looked rather tired. It's worth mentioning, however, that the color at least remained uniform — that is to say, there was no peeling, streaking or chipping in the finish. My conclusion was that deck stains certainly have their role: for something like a fence, deck or shed, they are a good solution.

ABOUT THE AUTHOR

Chris Gleason has owned and operated Gleason Woodworking Studio for over a decade. A self-taught craftsman, he specializes in contemporary furniture and kitchens.

With a degree in French from Vassar College in Poughkeepsie, New York, Chris had the opportunity to live and study abroad for a year in Switzerland. The mountain influence must have grabbed hold, as he now makes his home in Salt Lake City, Utah, where he mountain bikes and skis as much as possible. He is also an enthusiastic old-time banjo and fiddle player.

Chris is the author of a number of woodworking books, as well as *Backyard Projects for Today's Homestead.*

Read This Important Safety Notice

To prevent accidents, keep safety in mind while you work. Use the safety guards installed on power equipment; they are for your protection.

When working on power equipment, keep fingers away from saw blades, wear safety goggles to prevent injuries from flying wood chips and sawdust, wear hearing protection and consider installing a dust vacuum to reduce the amount of airborne sawdust in your woodshop.

Don't wear loose clothing, such as neckties or shirts with loose sleeves, or jewelry, such as rings, necklaces or bracelets, when working on power equipment. Tie back long hair to prevent it from getting caught in your equipment.

People who are sensitive to certain chemicals should check the chemical content of any product before using it.

Due to the variability of local conditions, construction materials, skill levels, etc., neither the author nor F+W Media assumes any responsibility for any accidents, injuries, damages or other losses incurred resulting from the material presented in this book.

The author and editors who compiled this book have tried to make the contents as accurate and correct as possible. Plans, illustrations, photographs and text have been carefully checked. All instructions, plans and projects should be carefully read, studied and understood before beginning construction.

Prices listed for supplies and equipment were current at the time of publication and are subject to change.

Acknowledgements

I'd like to take a minute to thank all of the people that I worked with during the creation of this book. I learned a lot by talking with other shed builders, and I learned just as much by working with my clients. The former taught me about techniques, and the latter provided me with interesting design challenges; both groups did a lot to further my understanding of the way that a thoughtfully planned and executed backyard building can enrich one's quality of life.

Acquisitions editor: David Thiel

Designer: Geoffrey Raker

Layout: Elyse Schwanke

Production coordinator: Mark Griffin

Metric Conversion Chart

TO CONVERT	TO	MULTIPLY BY
Inches	Centimeters	2.54
Centimeters	Inches	0.4
Feet	Centimeters	30.5
Centimeters	Feet	0.03
Yards	Meters	0.9
Meters	Yards	1.1

Distributed in Canada by Fraser Direct
100 Armstrong Avenue
Georgetown, Ontario L7G 5S4
Canada

Distributed in the U.K. and Europe by
F&W Media International, LTD
Brunel House, Ford Close
Newton Abbot
TQ12 4PU, UK
Tel: (+44) 1626 323200
Fax: (+44) 1626 323319
E-mail: enquiries@fwmedia.com

Distributed in Australia by Capricorn Link
P.O. Box 704
Windsor, NSW 2756
Australia

Visit our website at www.popularwoodworking.com or our consumer website at www.shopwoodworking.com for more woodworking information projects.

Other fine Popular Woodworking Books are available from your local bookstore or direct from the publisher.

16   15   14   13   12   5   4   3   2   1

fw media

Ideas. Instruction. Inspiration.

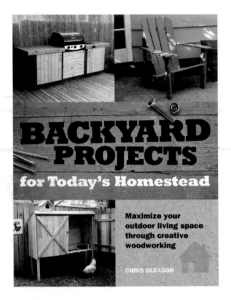